Developing Literacy WORD LEVEL

WORD-LEVEL ACTIVITIES FOR THE LITERACY HOUR

year

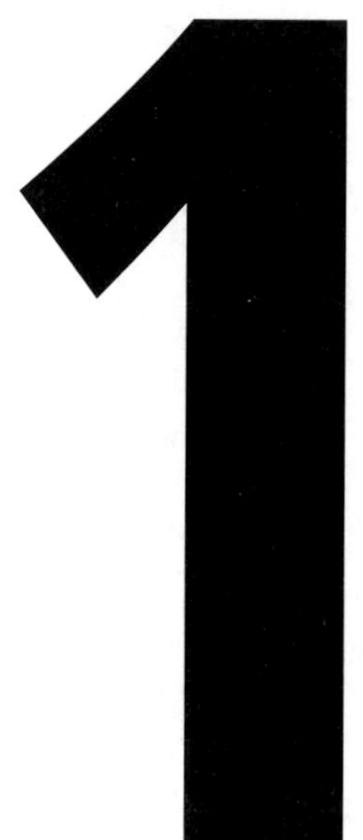

Ray Barker
Christine Moorcroft

A & C BLACK

Reprinted 1999 (three times), 2000
First published in 1998 by
A&C Black (Publishers) Limited
35 Bedford Row, London WC1R 4JH

ISBN 0-7136-4963-1

The authors and publishers would like to thank the following teachers for their advice in producing this series of books: Tracy Adam; Ann Hart; Lydia Hunt; Hazel Jacob; Madeleine Madden; Helen Mason; Yvonne Newman; Annette Norman; Katrin Trigg; Judith Wells.

A CIP catalogue record for this book is available from the British Library.

Printed in Great Britain by
St Edmundsbury Press Ltd, Bury St Edmunds, Suffolk.

Contents

Introduction

Developing Literacy: Word Level supports the teaching of reading and writing by providing a series of activities to develop essential skills in reading and spelling: word recognition and phonics. The activities are designed to be carried out in the time allocated to independent work during the Literacy Hour and therefore should be relatively 'teacher-free'. The focus is on children investigating words and spelling patterns, generating their own words in accordance with what they have learned and, if possible, recognising and devising rules and strategies to enable them to become independent in their recording and further investigation of language.

The activities presented in **Developing Literacy: Word Level** support the learning objectives of the National Literacy Strategy at word level. Each book

- includes activities which focus on phonics, spelling, word recognition and vocabulary;
- develops children's understanding of sound-spelling relationships;
- helps children to extend their vocabulary by challenging them to talk about and investigate the meanings of words which they find difficult;
- promotes independent work during the Literacy Hour;
- has extension activities on each page which reinforce and develop what the children have learned;
- includes brief notes for teachers at the bottom of most pages.

Some of the activities focus on the high frequency words listed in the National Literacy Strategy's *Framework for Teaching.* These are lists of words to be learned to be recognised on sight. At Key Stage 1, they are words which the children need to know in order to tackle even very simple texts. Some are regular but others, such as 'said' and 'water' do not follow regular phonic spelling patterns. At Key Stage 2, an additional list of medium frequency words is added which children often find difficulty in spelling.

The activities are presented in a way which requires children to read the words rather than just guessing the answers or 'filling in the spaces'. Sometimes they are asked to turn over the sheet and then write a list of words; a partner could read the words aloud for them to write. Working with partners or in groups is encouraged so that children can check one another's reading and co-operate to complete the activities or to play games. It is also useful for the children to show their work to the rest of the class and to explain their answers in order to reinforce and develop their own learning and that of others in the class.

Children need to 'Look, Say, Cover, Write and Check' (LSCWCh) words on a regular basis in order to learn their spellings. This has mostly been left to the teacher to initiate. However, it is used on some pages and is presented as follows:

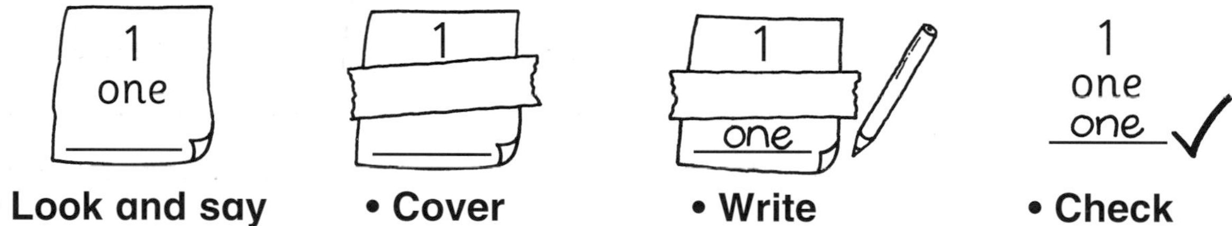

Extension

Each activity sheet ends with a challenge (**Now try this!**) which reinforces and extends the children's learning and provides the teacher with an opportunity for assessment. Where children are asked to carry out an activity, the instructions are clear to enable them to work independently. The teacher may decide to amend this before photocopying, depending on his or her knowledge of the children's abilities and speed of working, for example by reducing the number of words that the child is asked to write.

- **Trace the caterpillar.**
- **Write some different words on it.**

Organisation

For many of the activities it will be useful to have an easily accessible range of dictionaries, fiction and non-fiction books, coloured pencils, scissors and squared paper. Several activities can be re-used to provide more practice in different letters or sounds, by masking the words and/or letters and replacing them with others of your choice, such as on page 9.

To help teachers to select appropriate learning experiences for their pupils, the activities are grouped into sections within each book. The pages are **not** intended to be presented in the order in which they appear in the books. The teacher should select the appropriate pages to support the work in progress. Some children may be weak in areas which were covered in previous years. If so, teachers can refer to the **Developing Literacy: Word Level** book for the previous year to find appropriate activity sheets, which may be adapted, to practise those areas. For more able children, the teacher may want to adapt the activity sheets by masking the words and letters and replacing them with more demanding examples.

Many activities will be completed entirely on the activity sheets. For others, particularly in the extension activities, the children will need to work either on the back of the page, on a separate sheet of paper or in an exercise book.

It is useful for children to keep their own **word banks** with the new words they have learnt. These could be general or for a specific theme on which the class is working, such as animals. Children should be encouraged to make a note of any words they cannot read so that they can add them to the word bank. The class could also have a **word wall** display to which they can add new words.

Structure of the Literacy Hour

The recommended structure of the Literacy Hour for Key Stage 1 is as follows:

Whole class introduction	**15 min**	Shared text work (balance of reading and writing) in which the teacher reads or writes a piece of text with the class, to elicit the children's participation in discussion of the topic to be taught.
Whole class activity	**15 min**	Focused word work in which the children contribute to a teacher-led activity arising from the whole class introduction
Group work **Independent work (rest of class)**	**20 min**	The teacher works with groups of children on guided text work. The other children could work independently, for example, from an activity in one of the **Developing Literacy** series (**Word Level**, **Sentence Level** or **Text Level**).
Whole class plenary session	**10 min**	The teacher leads a review of what has been learned by consolidating teaching points, reviewing, reflecting and sharing the children's ideas and the results of their work in the lesson.

The following flow chart shows an example of the way in which an activity from this book can be used to achieve the required organisation of the Literacy Hour.

Alphabet caterpillar a to m and **Alphabet caterpillar n to z** (pages 9–10)

Whole class introduction **15 min**
Read a book which features the letters of the alphabet, such as *I Spy: Alphabet of Art* by Lucy Micklethwait (HarperCollins), inviting the children to join in the 'I spy' activity about each picture.

Whole class activity **15 min**
Have a large 'alphabet caterpillar' on a displayboard to which the children can contribute their own words.

Group work **20 min**
The teacher works with groups of children to produce alphabets with themes such as sports and games or food; the children use dictionaries to find words, within the topic, which begin with each letter of the alphabet.

Independent work **20 min**
The rest of the children work on **Alphabet caterpillar** (pages 9 and 10) from **Developing Literacy: Word Level Year 1**.

Whole class plenary session **10 min**
The children share their ideas, adding to the giant 'alphabet caterpillar', by referring to the worksheet they have done or the alphabets with themes they have prepared while working in a group with a teacher.

Teachers' notes

Very brief notes are provided at the end of most pages. They give ideas and suggestions for maximising the effectiveness of the activity sheets. They may make suggestions for the whole-class introduction, the plenary session or for follow-up work using an adapted version of the activity sheet.

Before photocopying, these notes could be masked.

Teachers' note During the plenary session, the children could play a verbal game in which they add anything they like, however silly, to the containers, for example, 'In my jar I have jelly, jam, jewels, James, a jaguar...'.	**Developing Literacy** **Word Level Year 1** **© A & C Black 1998**

Teachers' note Provide a collection of diaries and calendars. Encourage the children to read the names of the days of the week in different text styles and layouts.	**Developing Literacy** **Word Level Year 1** **© A & C Black 1998**

Using the activity sheets

Brief information is given here about the work within each section of **Developing Literacy: Word Level Year 1**. Suggestions are also given for additional activities.

Alphabetical order (pages 9–13)

This section supports the learning of the names of the letters and their order in the alphabet and teaches children how alphabetical order can be useful. It helps them to learn to recognise and use upper- and lower-case letters.

Vowels (pages 14–16)

The activities in this section help children to learn which letters are vowels and how they are used in words.

You could reinforce the recognition of 'vowels' and 'consonants' by playing 'Snap' with the children. Write each letter of the alphabet on a separate card about the size of a playing card, making three copies of each vowel. The children deal the cards and then take turns to put down a card. Any player can call 'Snap' when the card just played shows the same type of letter (vowel or consonant) as the previous card. If correct, they take all the cards played. Players drop out of the game when they have lost all their cards. The winner finishes with all the cards.

You could also show 'flash cards' of words, and ask the children to identify the vowels. Ask the children to write or word-process their names, without the vowels, on strips of paper. Display the names. Can they recognise one another's names?

High frequency words (pages 17-27)

This section helps children with word recognition. Space does not allow all the words on the National Literacy Strategy's list for Year 1 to appear in these activities, but many of the activities can be adapted for use with other words.

Word work 1 and **Word work 4** (pages 17 and 20) draw children's attention to the shapes of words, thus developing a useful strategy to help with word recognition. It focuses on letters with ascenders or descenders or neither. The teacher can provide similar activities to encourage sight-reading of other words on the National Literacy Strategy's recommended list of high frequency words by drawing the shapes of words on squared paper. For group or class demonstrations, use paper printed with large squares. Provide the children with paper marked into large squares and ask them to draw and cut out the shapes of words (provide a list of three to five words). Ask them to pass their shapes to a partner, together with the list of words, so that the partner can write the words in the appropriate shapes.

Word work 2, 3, 5 and 6 (pages 18, 19, 21 and 22) are activities which require children to distinguish between a small number of words from the high frequency list.

The purpose of the activities on pages 23 to 26 is to teach the spellings of the numbers from one to twenty and the days of the week. The children could also look at calendars and diaries and copy the different ways in which numbers and days are written.

Family word bank (page 27) focuses on the spelling of family words. It is just one idea for vocabulary extension by making word collections linked to particular topics. Provide appropriate formats on which the children can make word collections for other topics, for example, a pirate's hat for words about pirates, a cat for words about pets, and so on.

Onset and rime (pages 28–39)

The activities in this section teach children to break down words into their beginning sound (onset) and the part which follows (rime) and to recognise when words have the same beginning sounds.

In **Cars and roads** (page 28), the children learn to make a simple consonant-vowel-consonant (CVC) word. The cars could be enlarged using a photocopier and then cut out and arranged in three 'roads' (initial consonant, middle vowel and final consonant). The children could be asked to make words using a car from each road. To provide more practice, mask the letters on the cars before copying them and write other letters in their place.

Beginning sounds b, j, p, s (page 29) and **Beginning sounds c, d, t, v** (page 30) help the children to tackle new words by focusing on their initial sounds.

The activities in **Word endings** (pages 31 to 34) and **Making new words** (pages 35-36) teach the children to discriminate the initial consonant from the rest of the word and to blend phonemes to form CVC words. Each page ends with a challenge to make a silly sentence with words which fall into given patterns.

In **Jigsaw words** (page 37) and the **Word spinner game** (pages 38–39) the children learn to discriminate between the initial sound and the rest of a word. They also practise blending phonemes to form words. These pages also reinforce common spelling patterns.

Phonemes (pages 40–47)

Teachers should be aware that in some areas the regional accent will affect the sound which a phoneme makes, for example the short **a** used in bath and path in Northern areas.

In **End sounds** (page 40), the children's attention is focused on the final consonants of CVC words. Further practice can be provided by asking the children to cut out and collect from catalogues and magazines pictures of things which end with a given consonant sound. They could then be glued on to an 'ends in **t**' page or an 'ends in **d**' page.

Bees, Boots and **Rain** (pages 41–43) help the children to recognise the common spelling patterns of long vowel phonemes. In **Finding phonemes** (pages 44–45), the emphasis is on saying the words and listening to the sounds. They provide practice for the children in recognising sounds which are the same, whether or not they are spelled in the same way, for example, 'plate' and 'drain', 'feet' and 'beans', 'pies' and 'pipe'.

Plurals with s (page 46) introduces straightforward plurals which are formed by adding **s**.

y endings (page 47) teaches children to recognise long **y** sounds, at the ends of words, where **y** is used as a vowel.

Names (pages 48–49)

The children will have practised writing their names during the Reception year. This section reinforces previous learning while providing practice in recognising initial phonemes and in the spelling and recognition of high frequency words.

Name wall (page 48) and **Words in names** (page 49) provide reinforcement of the spellings of the children's own names and other names in the class. They also teach children to use capital letters to start names and provide practice in recognition and spelling of other words which the children use frequently.

Rhymes (pages 50–53)

In this section the children learn to recognise similar-sounding words by using rhymes. They learn that the same sounds can be spelled in different ways. In **Rhyme trees** (page 50) and **Make a rhyme** (page 51), the children develop spelling skills by reading and writing rhymes with the same spelling, for example, cat, hat, bat.

Double consonants (pages 54–57)

The children investigate, read and spell words which end with the double consonants **ll, ff** and **ss**. The letter string **ck** is also regarded as a double consonant because the letters make the same sound. When they find words ending in **-all**, ask them what they notice about the way in which adding **ll** changes the sound of **a**.

Initial consonant clusters (pages 58–64)

In these activities the children learn to discriminate between, read and spell words with similar initial consonant clusters. After completing the activities they could play 'I spy' in small groups or as a class. For more able children you could use the endings of words rather than the beginnings. The teacher could provide pictures of objects whose names have the final clusters which the children will practise.

The **Teachers' notes** at the bottom of each page in this section suggest that before working on each activity, in the whole class introduction, a shared text is used which has some of the initial consonant clusters being studied on that page. A suggestion is often given of an appropriate nursery rhyme or story which could be used. This could be written on a large sheet of paper or the board, or a text could be selected from a big book. Some of the rhymes suggested are old rhymes which may not be familiar, and so they are provided below. The rhymes printed below have been marked with an asterisk in the **Teachers' notes.**

Useful rhymes and jingles

Ten Green Bottles
Old MacDonald had a Farm
There was an Old Lady who Swallowed a Fly
Twinkle, Twinkle, Little Star
Pat-a-Cake, Pat-a-Cake
Bye, Baby Bunting
Ding, Dong, Bell
Mary, Mary, Quite Contrary
Wee Willie Winkie
Jack and Jill

My Father was a Frenchman
My Father was a Frenchman
A Frenchman, a Frenchman
My Father was a Frenchman
And he bought me a fiddle
He cut it here
He cut it there
He cut it through the middle.

The Crooked Man
There was a crooked man,
Who walked a crooked mile,
And found a crooked sixpence
Against a crooked stile;
He bought a crooked cat,
Which caught a crooked mouse,
And they all lived together
In a little crooked house.

Gregory Griggs
Gregory Griggs, Gregory Griggs
Had twenty-seven different wigs.
He wore them up, he wore them down,
To please the people of the town;
He wore them east, he wore them west,
But he could not tell which he liked best.

Swan swim
Swan swim over the sea,
Swim, swan, swim!
Swan swam back again,
Well swum swan!

Glossary of terms used

analogy Recognising a word, phoneme or pattern in known words and applying it to new, unfamiliar words.
ascender The part of a letter which projects upwards, for example in **b, d, h** and **k**.
blending Running together individual phonemes in pronunciation.
cluster A combination of consonant sounds before or after a vowel (or **y** used as a vowel); for example, **spr**ay, **cr**y, ru**st**.
descender The part of a letter which projects downwards, for example in **g, j, p** and **y**.
onset The initial consonant or consonant cluster of a word or syllable; for example, **tr**ain, **scr**ape, **sk**ate.
phoneme The smallest unit of sound in a word. A phoneme can be represented by one to four letters; for example, thi**n**, thi**ck**, th**igh**, th**ough**.
phonics The relationship between sounds and the written form of a language.
rhyme The use of words which have the same sound in their final syllable; for example, f**ox**/r**ocks**, s**ore**/d**oor**.
rime The part of a word or syllable which contains the vowel and final consonant or consonant cluster, for example, sh**eep**, sl**ow**, f**oal**.
syllable A rhythmic segment of a word; for example, **can** (1 syllable) , **car- ton** (2 syllables)

Alphabet caterpillar a to m

- **Read the words on the leaf.**
- **Look at their first letters.**
- **Copy them on to the caterpillar.**

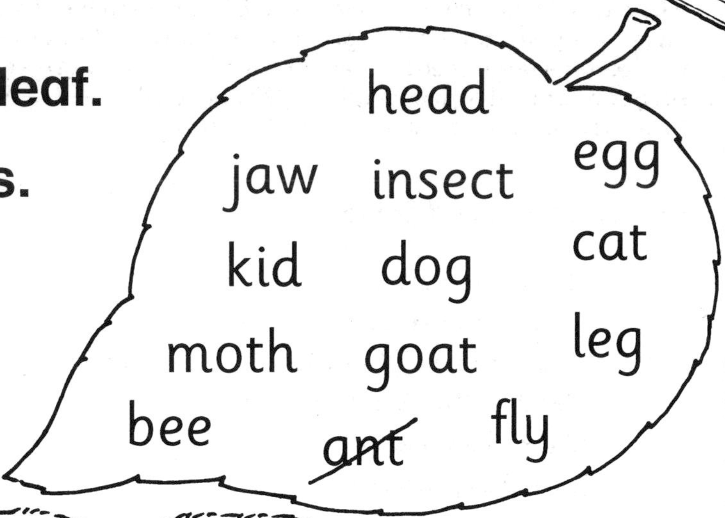

head
jaw insect egg
kid dog cat
moth goat leg
bee ~~ant~~ fly

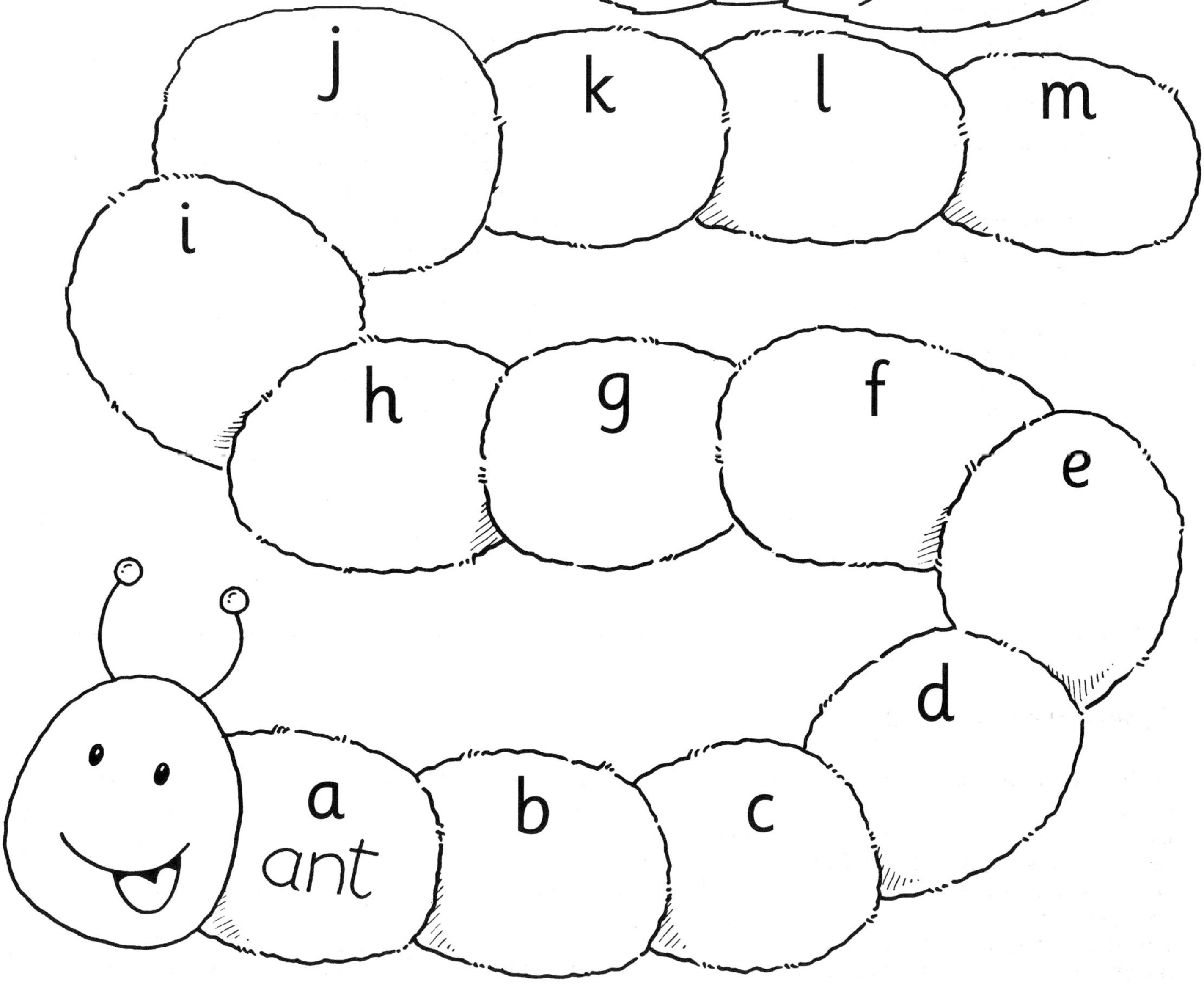

j k l m
i
h g f
e
d
a b c
ant

- **Trace the caterpillar.**
- **Write some different words on it.**

Teachers' note Encourage the children to make a note of any words they can not read. For more practice, mask the words provided and replace them with words of your own choice.

Alphabet caterpillar n to z

- Read the words on the leaf.
- Look at their first letters.
- Copy them on to the caterpillar.

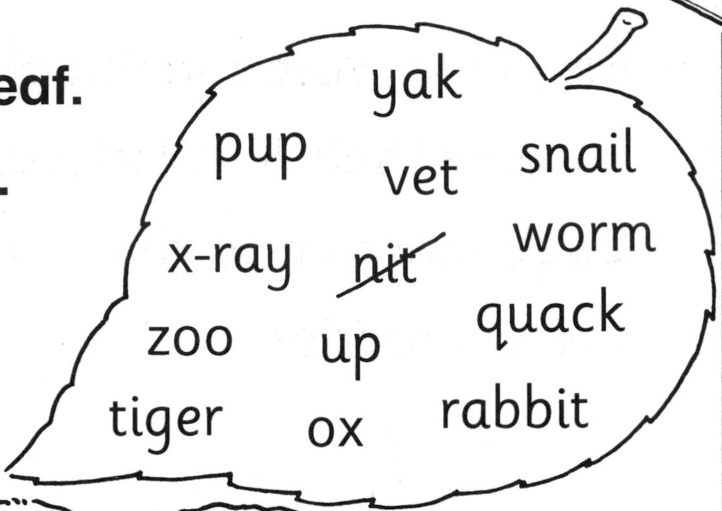

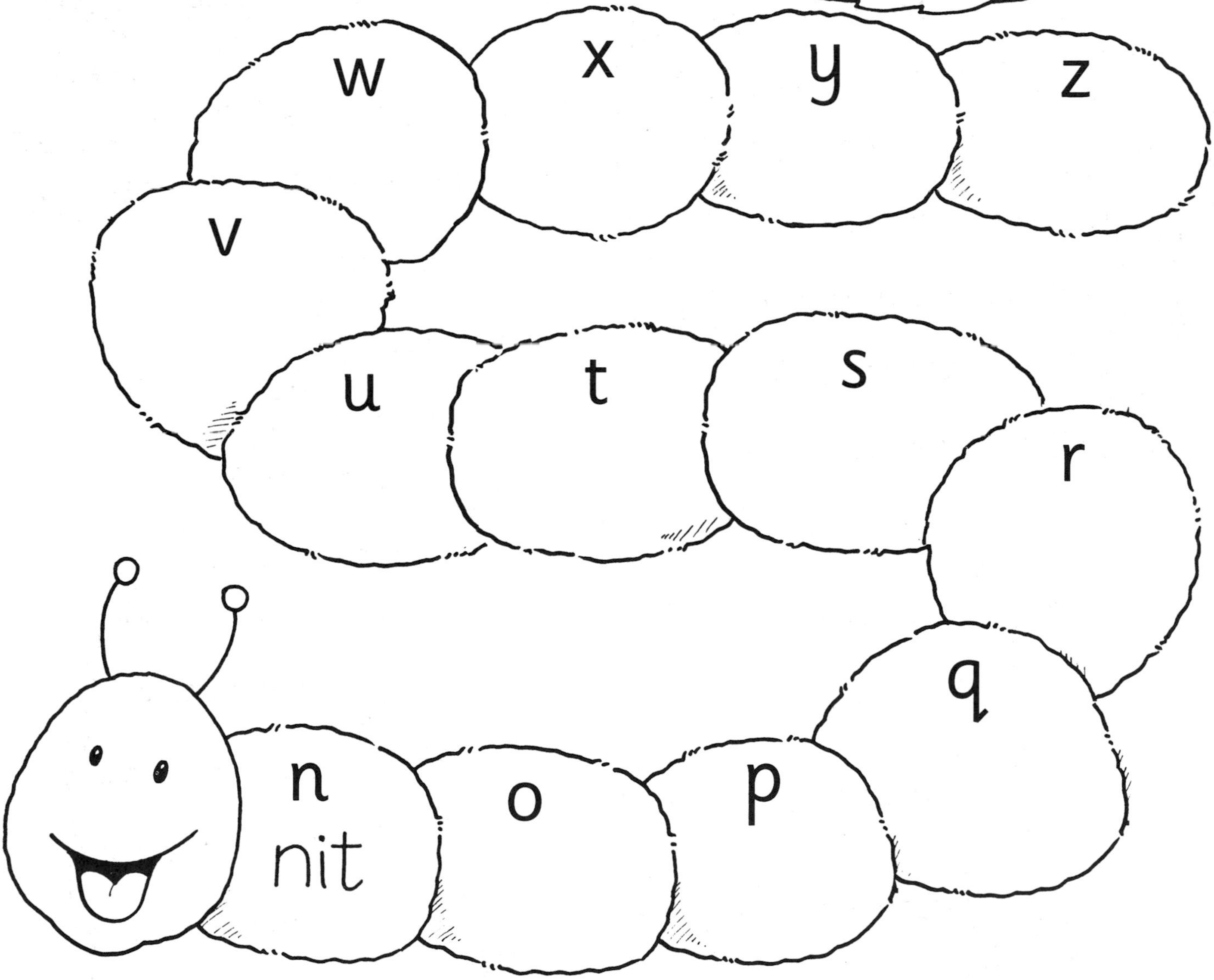

- Trace the caterpillar.
- Write some different words on it.

Teachers' note Encourage the children to make a note of any words they can not read. For more practice, mask the words provided and replace them with words of your own choice.

Aa to Mm

- **Read the words in the cloud.**
- **Look at their first letters.**
- **Copy them on to the correct ladder.**

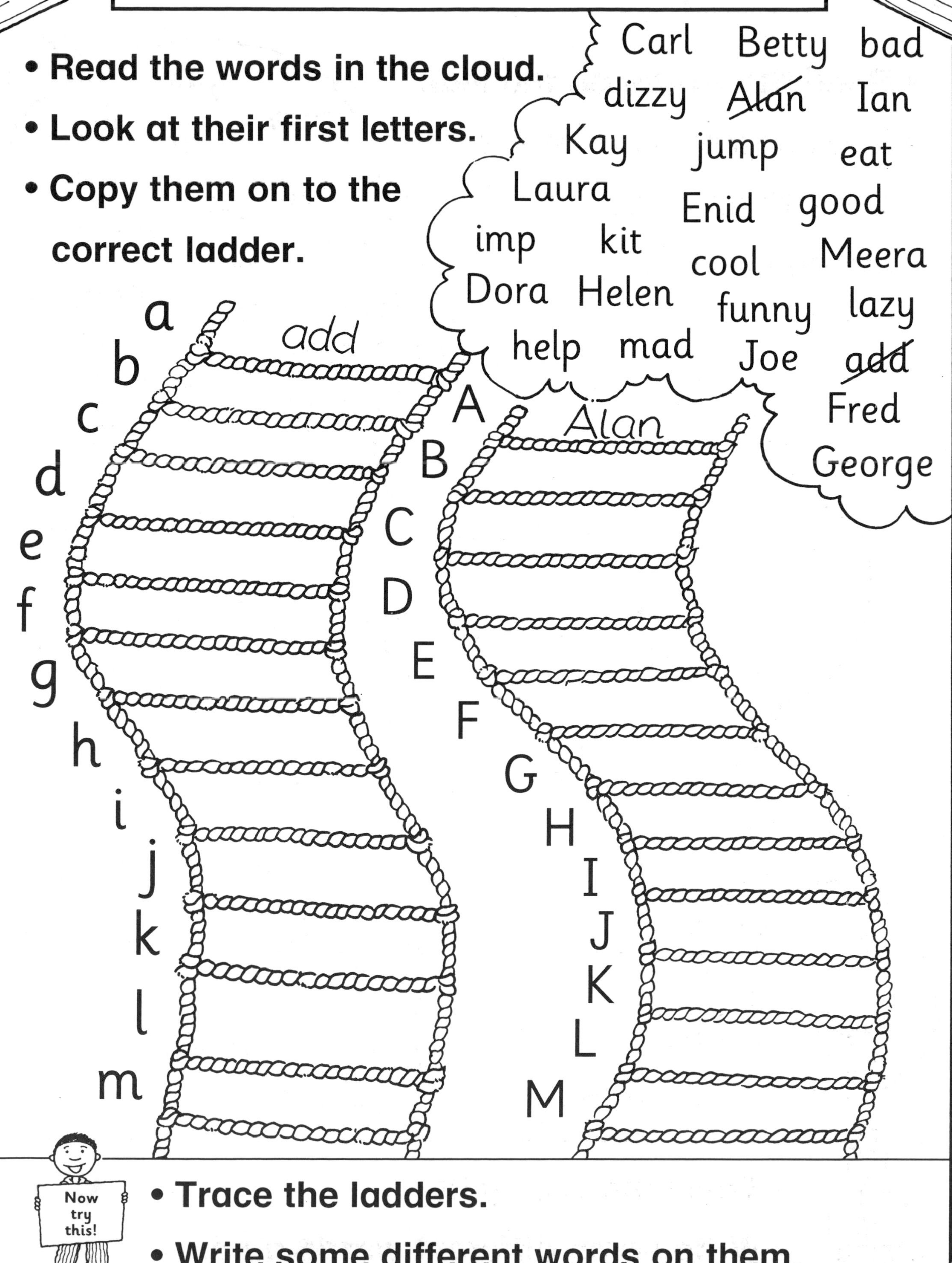

- **Trace the ladders.**
- **Write some different words on them.**

Teachers' note Encourage the children to make a note of any words they can not read. For more practice, mask the words provided and replace them with words of your own choice.

Nn to Zz

- Read the words in the cloud.
- Look at their first letters.
- Copy them on to the correct ladder.

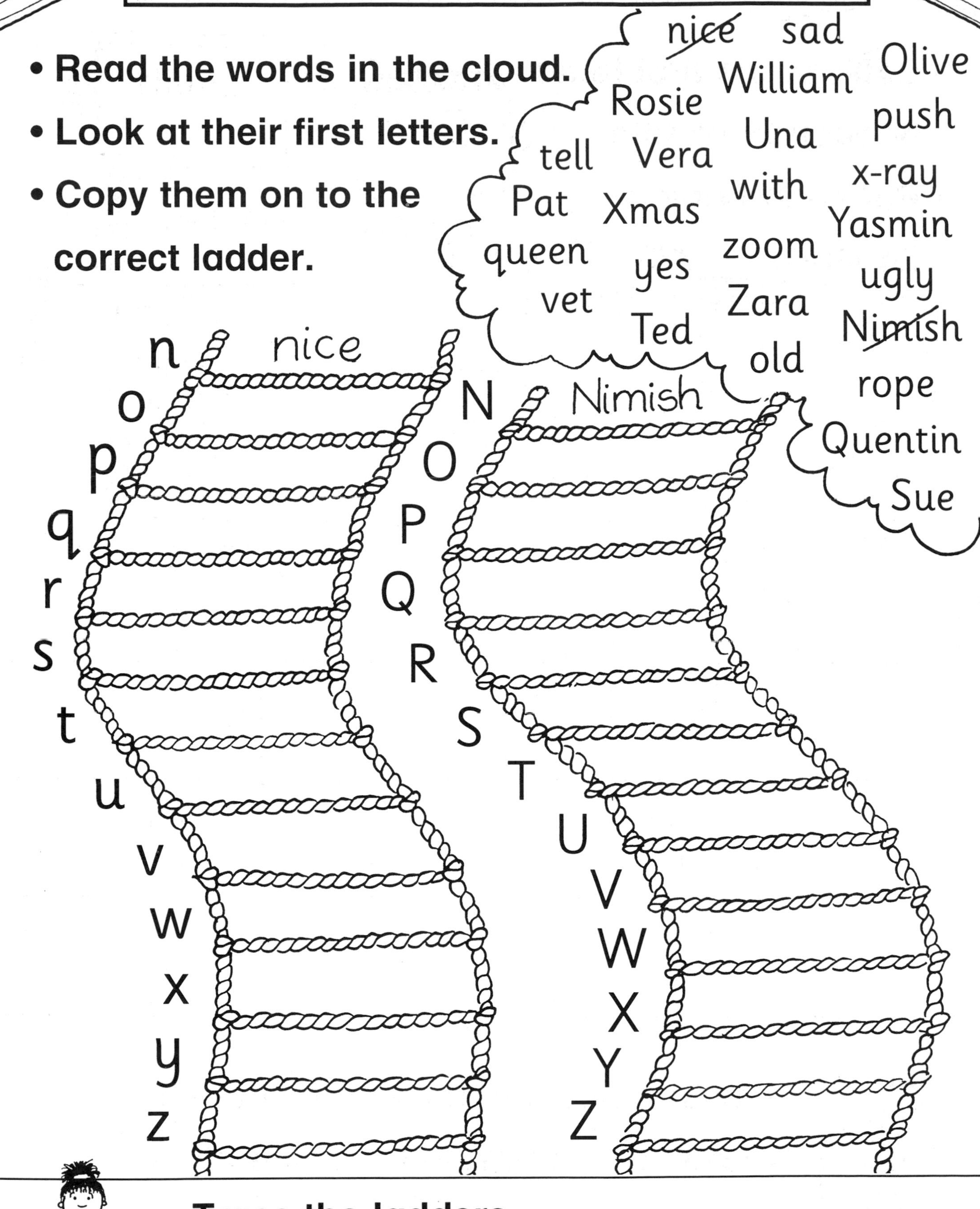

- Trace the ladders.
- Write some different words on them.

Teachers' note Encourage the children to make a note of any words they can not read. For more practice, mask the words provided and replace them with words of your own choice.

Bookshelf

- **Look at the first letter of each book title.**
- **Put each book on its shelf.**

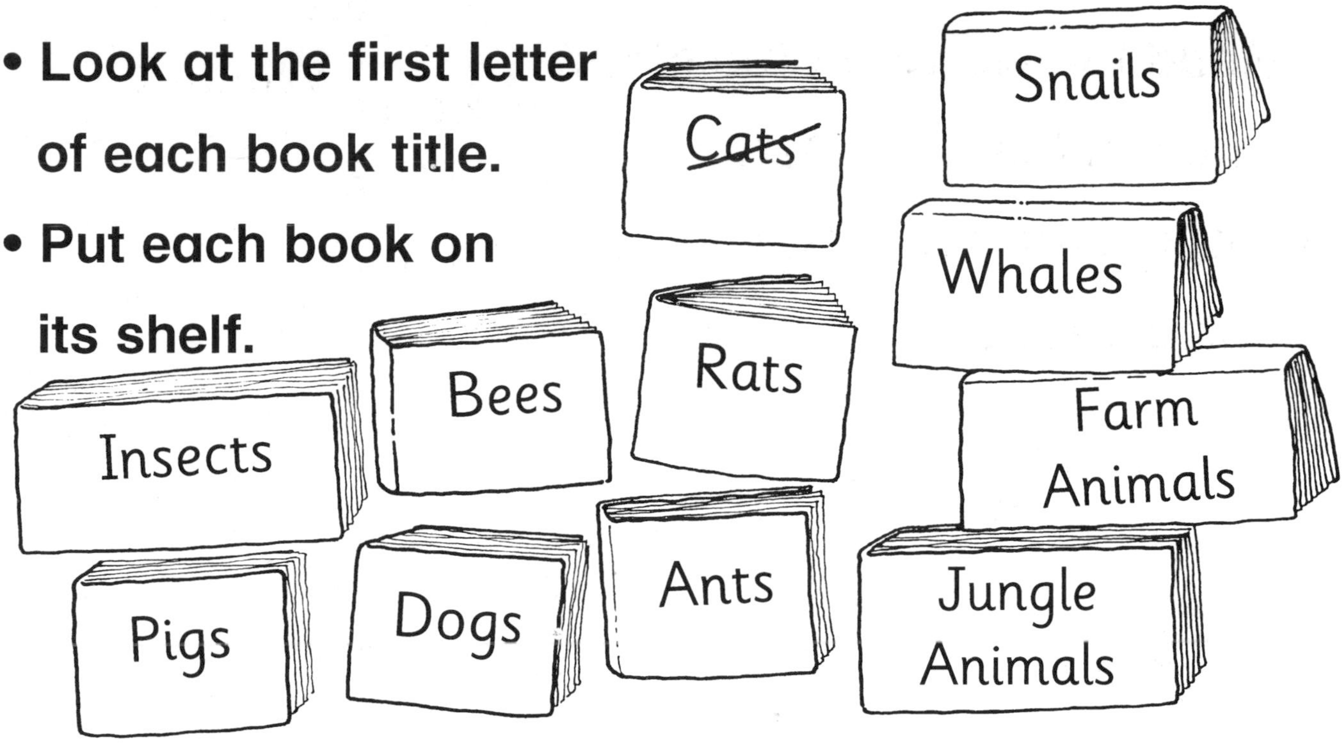

~~Cats~~ Snails Whales Rats Bees Insects Farm Animals Pigs Dogs Ants Jungle Animals

A		B		C	Cats	D		E	

F		G		H		I		J	

K		L		M		N		O		P		Q	

R		S		T		U V W		X Y Z	

- **With a partner, collect ten books.**
- **Look at the first letter of the titles.**
- **Decide on which of the A to Z shelves they belong.**

Teachers' note Children who complete this extension successfully could put a collection of ten books (possibly the same collection) in alphabetical order by authors' surnames.

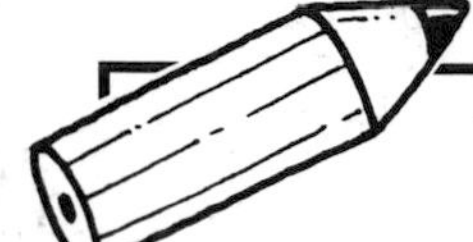

Vowel shopping

These letters are vowels.

a e i o u

- **Say their names.**
- **Underline the vowels in the shopping.**

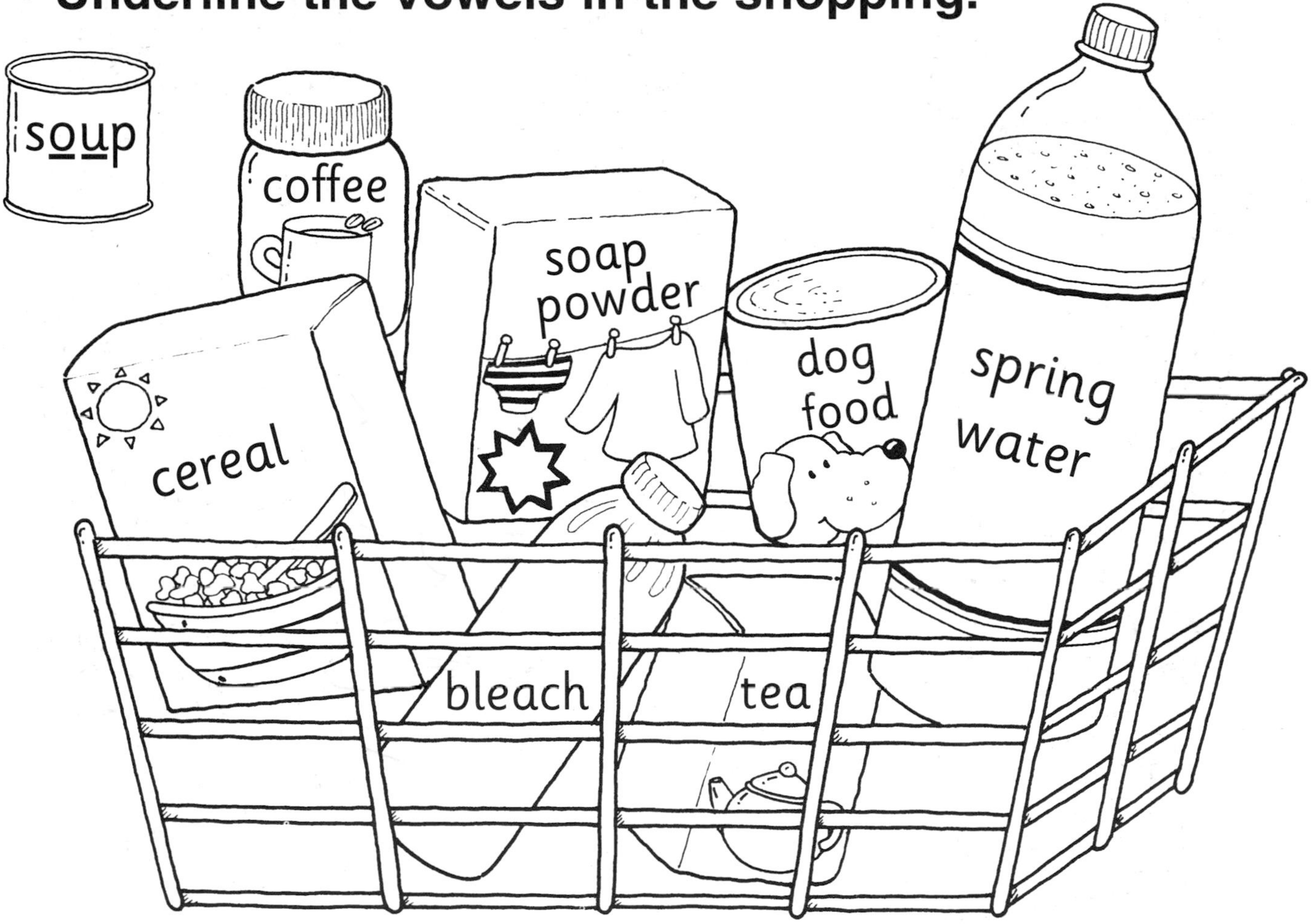
soup
coffee
soap powder
cereal
dog food
spring water
bleach
tea

- **Write your name.**

Kate

- **Underline the vowels.**

Now try this!

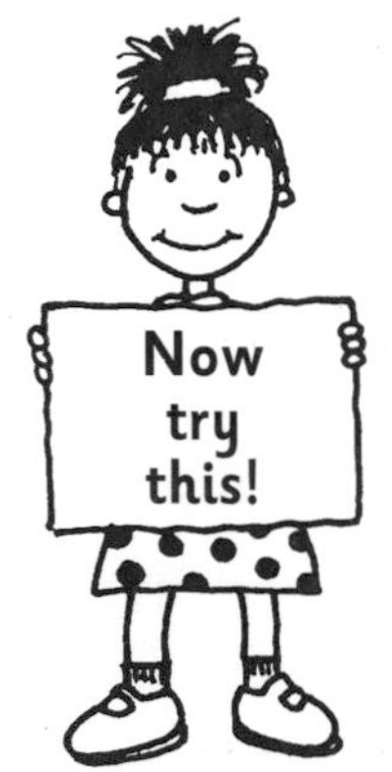

- **Write your friends' names.**
- **Underline the vowels.**

Teachers' note The children could copy the names of foods and other items from their labels, putting dashes to represent the vowels, for a partner to complete.

Vowel flags

- Choose a vowel for each word.
- Complete the word.

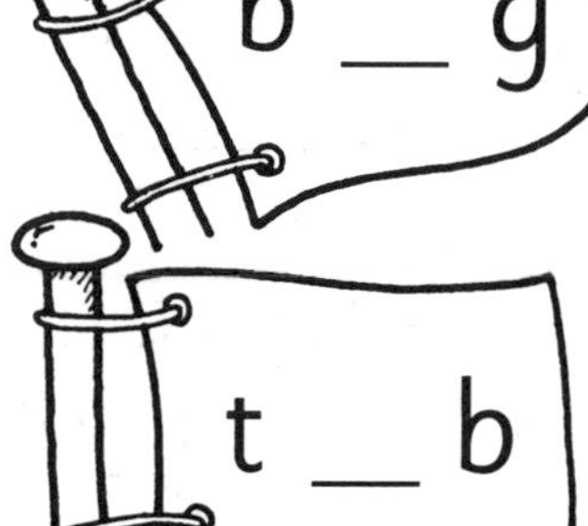

t _ b

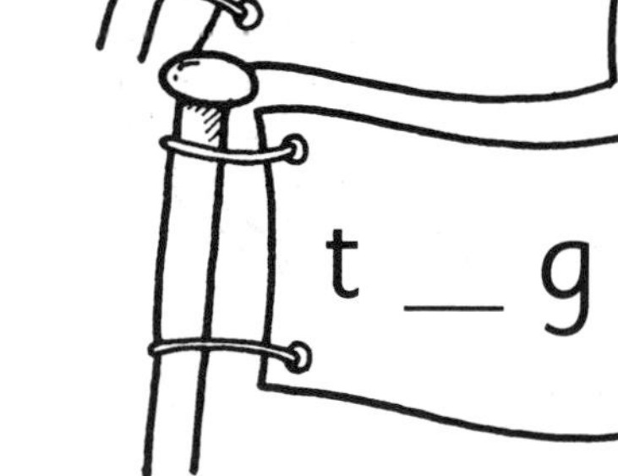

t _ g

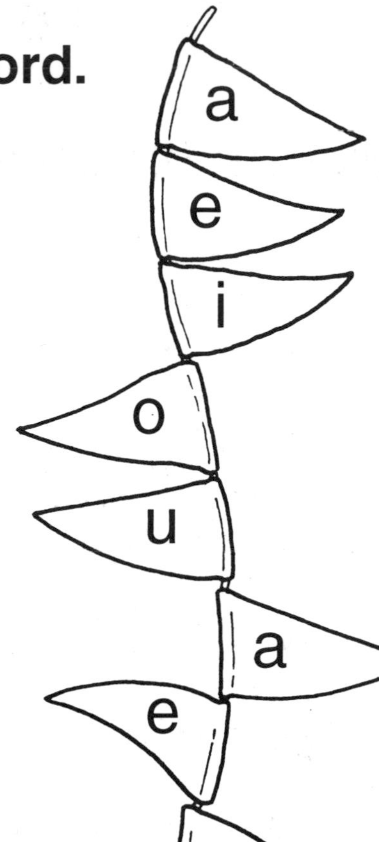

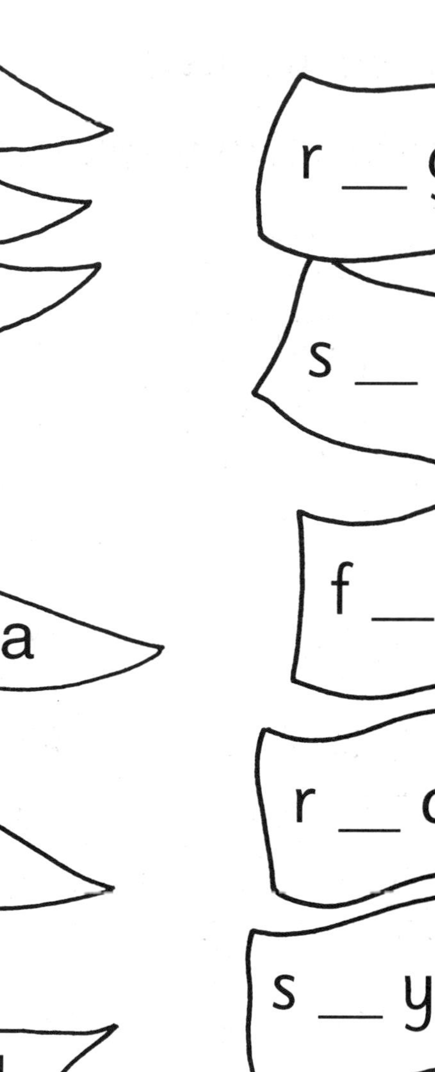

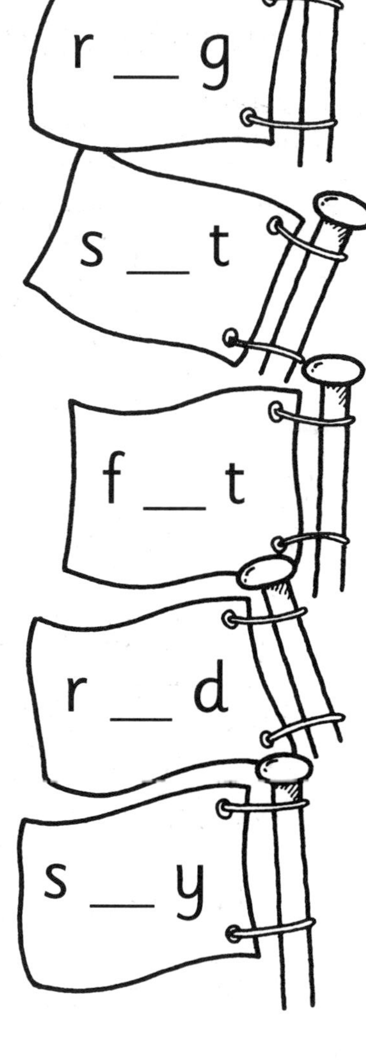

- Write the words you have made.

rip ______ ______ ______ ______

______ ______ ______ ______ ______

- Change the vowels. Write the new words.

rap ______ ______ ______ ______

______ ______ ______ ______ ______

Teachers' note You or the children could make some large flags by gluing paper to art straws. The children could write words with their vowels missing for a partner to complete.

Vowel change

- **Add the correct vowel.**

- **Change the vowel.**
- **Make a new word.**

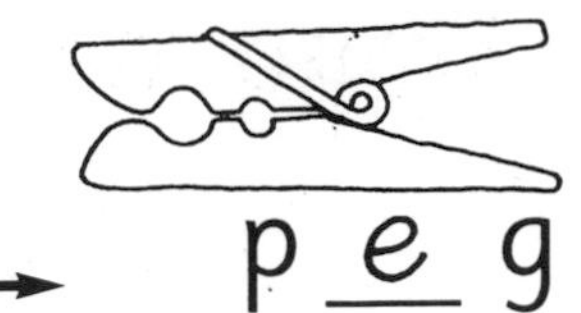

p i g → p e g

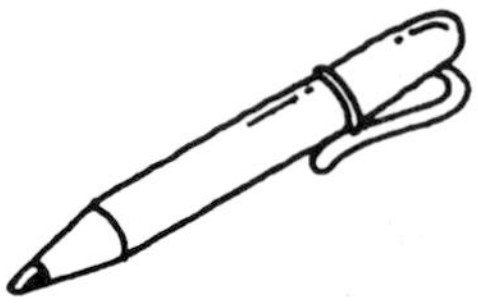  p _ n → p _ n	  c _ t → c _ t
 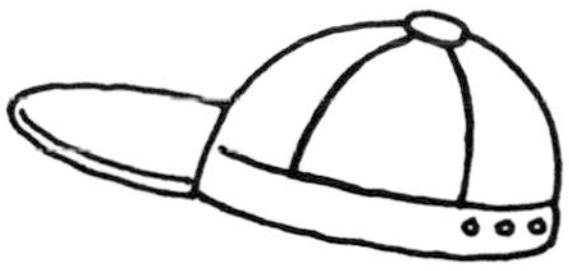 c _ p → c _ p	  b _ n → b _ n
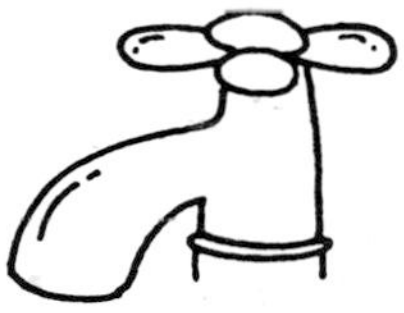  t _ p → t _ p	  h _ t → h _ t
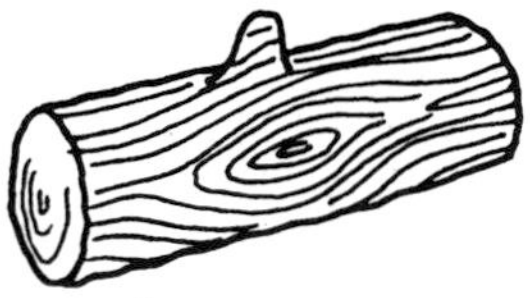 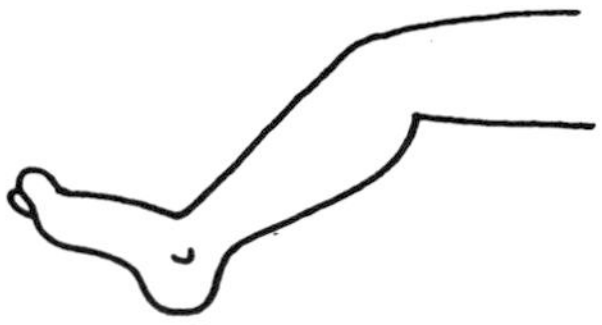 l _ g → l _ g	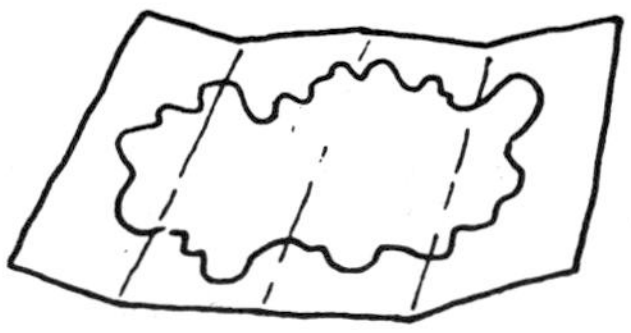 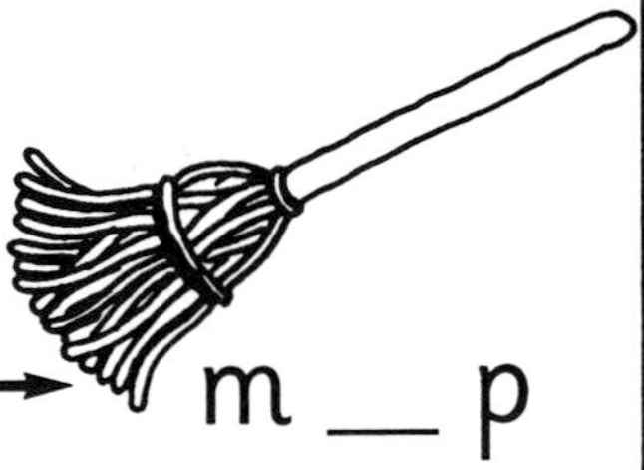 m _ p → m _ p

- **Copy these words.**
- **Change the vowels.**
- **Write the new words.**

net	pip
pot	rod
rag	ten

- **List six other words and change the vowels.**

Teachers' note Introduce the activity by writing a consonant-vowel-consonant (CVC) word on the board. Ask the children to suggest new words by changing the vowel.

Word work 1

- **Write the words in the shapes.**

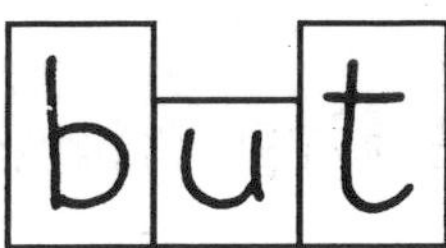

back ball be bed

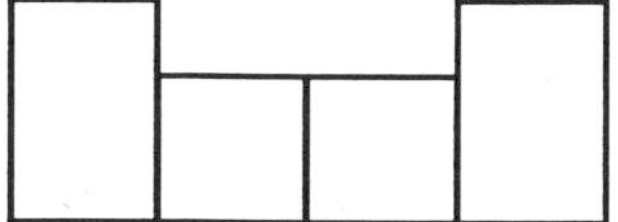
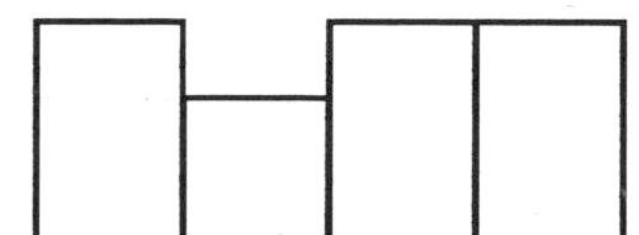
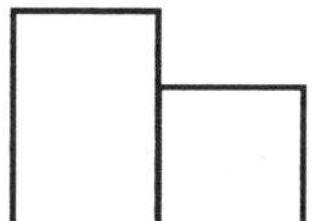

- **Complete the sentences with the words above.**

Come 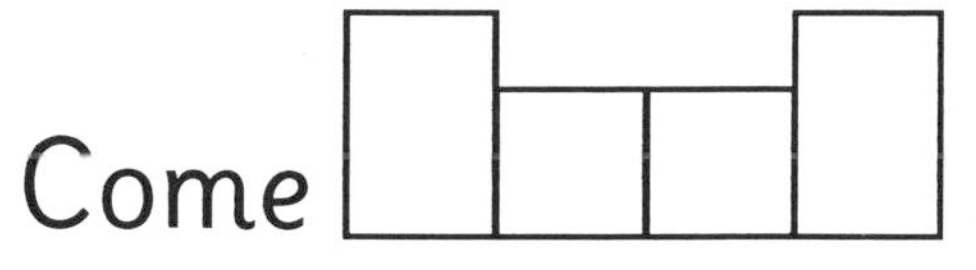. I will ☐☐ good.

Go to 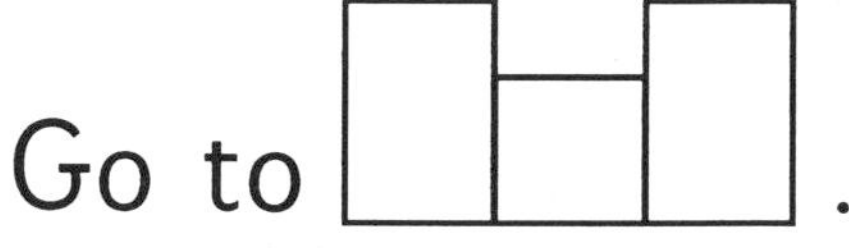. Hit the ☐☐☐☐.

- **Write back, ball, be or bed in the sentences.**

Will you ______ late? Go ______ home.

Kick the ______. I sleep in a ______ .

- **Turn over this page.**
- **Without copying, write these words.**

back ball be bed

Teachers' note The children can copy these word shapes on to squared paper and then think of other words which will fit into them.

Word work 2

- **Read these words.**

an	another	as	back

- **Find these words in the shapes on this page.**
- **Colour the shapes using these colours.**

an – red another – brown

as – blue back – yellow

- **Look in books for these words.**

an	another	as	back

- **Read the sentences you find with these words in.**
- **Write a new sentence for each word.**

Teachers' note Introduce the activity by discussing the meaning of the words and use the words in a sentence.

Word work 3

- **Read these words.**

after again about

- **Colour the shapes using these colours.**

after – blue again – green about – red

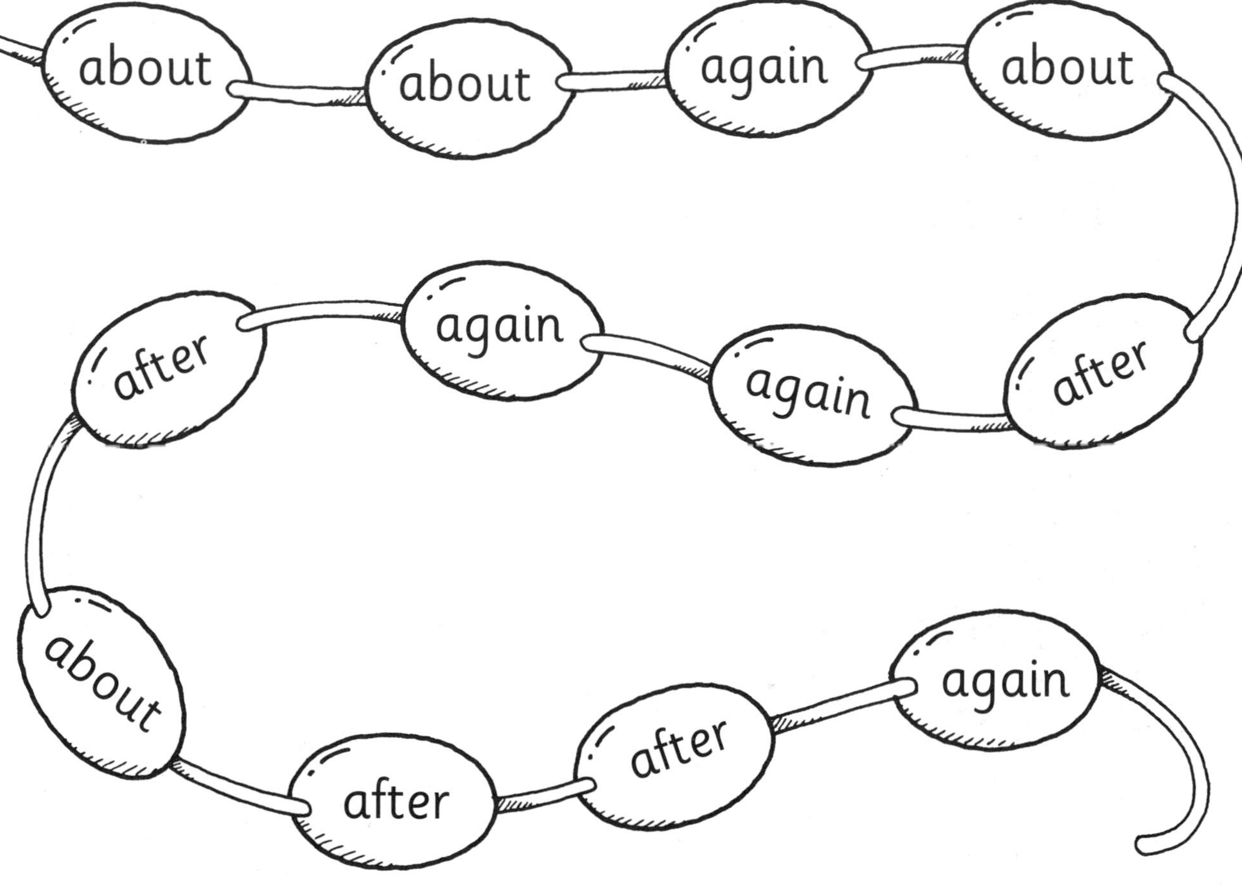

- **Write a sentence for each of these words.**

after again about

- **Without copying, write these words.**

after again about

Teachers' note Encourage the children to listen to and look at the second phoneme of each word. They all begin with **a**, but the second phoneme in each word is different.

Word work 4

- **Write the words in the shapes.**

going away play

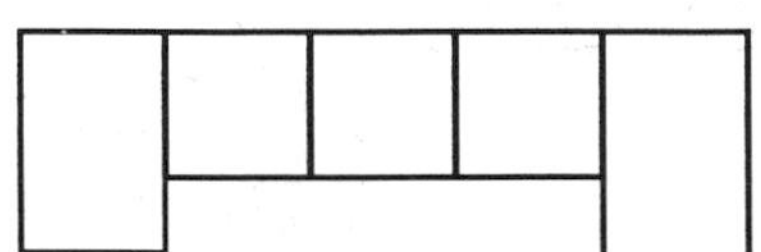
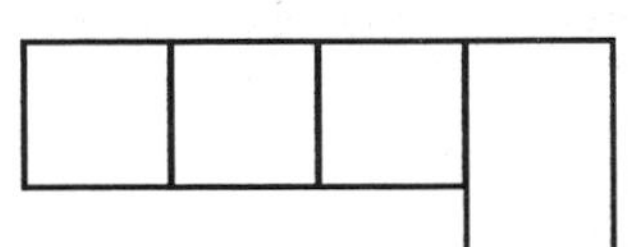
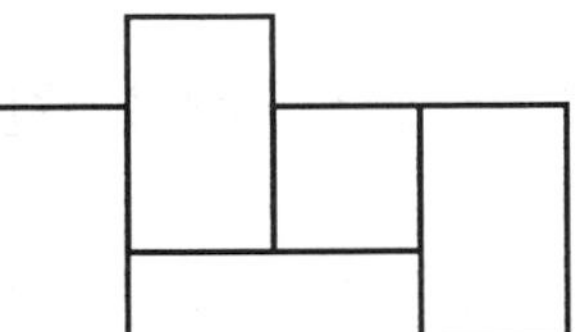

- **Complete the sentences with the words above.**

I am 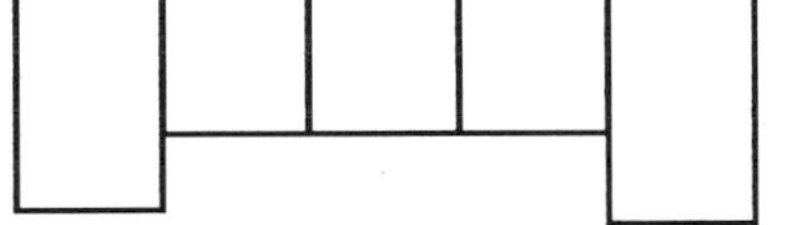 .

Go ______ .

I can 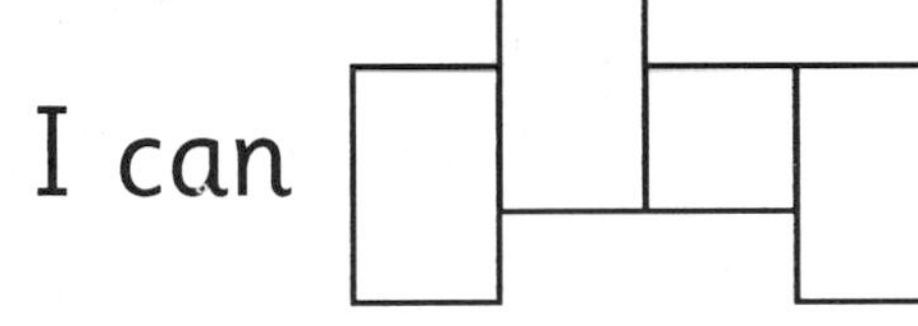 football.

- **Write** going **,** away **or** play **in the sentences.**

Jan went ______ .

I ______ with Anhil.

I am ______ to France.

- **Turn over this page.**
- **Without copying, write these words.**

going away play

Teachers' note Ask the children how away and play are similar (both end with **ay**). Can they think of other words with the same endings?

Word work 5

- **Read these words.**

because | been | boy | brother | but

- **Colour the shapes using these colours.**

because – red
boy – green
but – purple
been – blue
brother – yellow

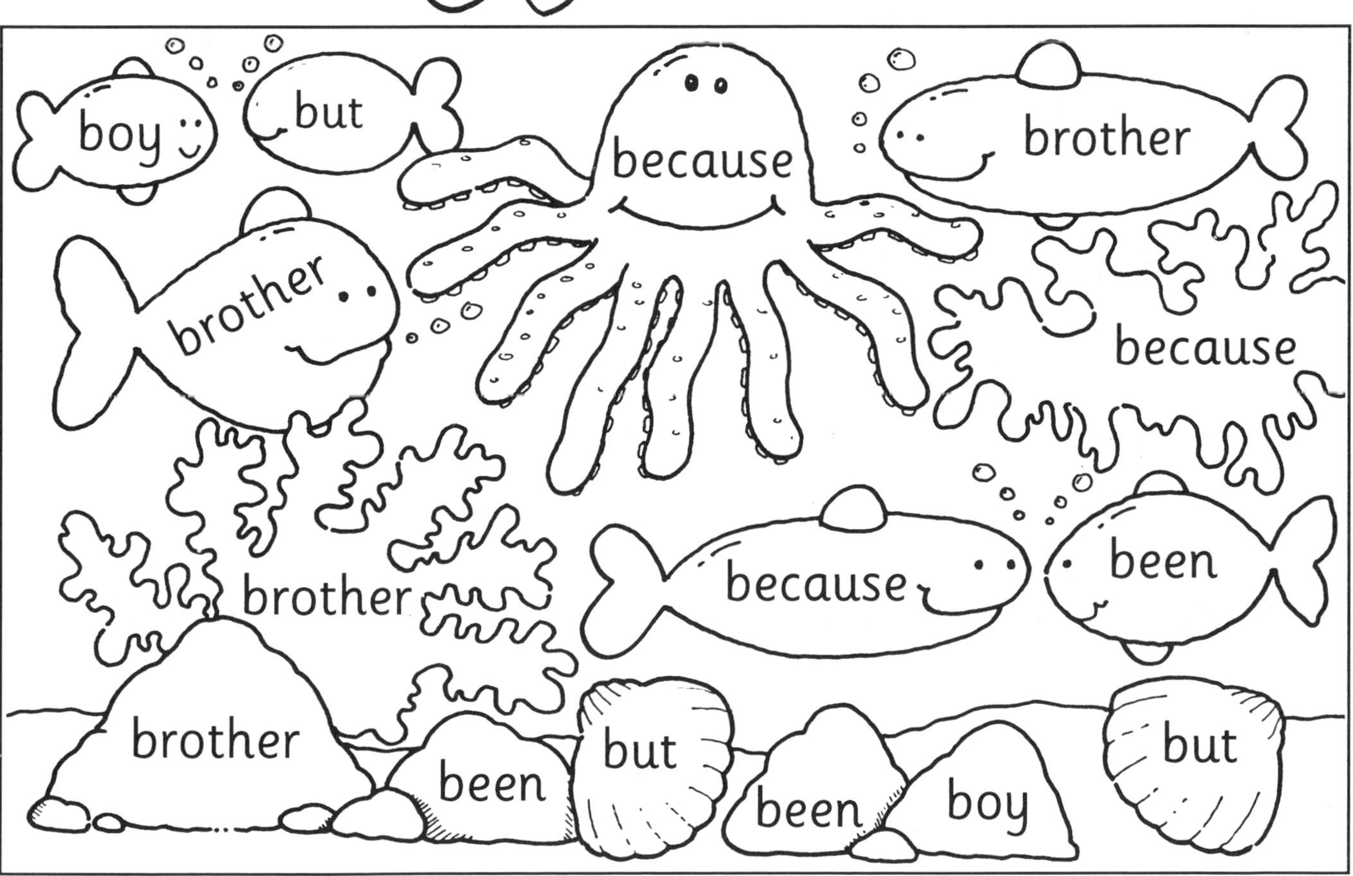

- **Write sentences for these words.**

because | been | boy | brother | but

- **Without copying, write these words.**

because | been | boy | brother | but

Teachers' note The children could write these, and other words which they have met in the **Word work** section, on to their own personal word banks.

Word work 6

- **Read these words.**

- **Colour the shapes using these colours.**

came – blue   call – red

can – green   by – yellow

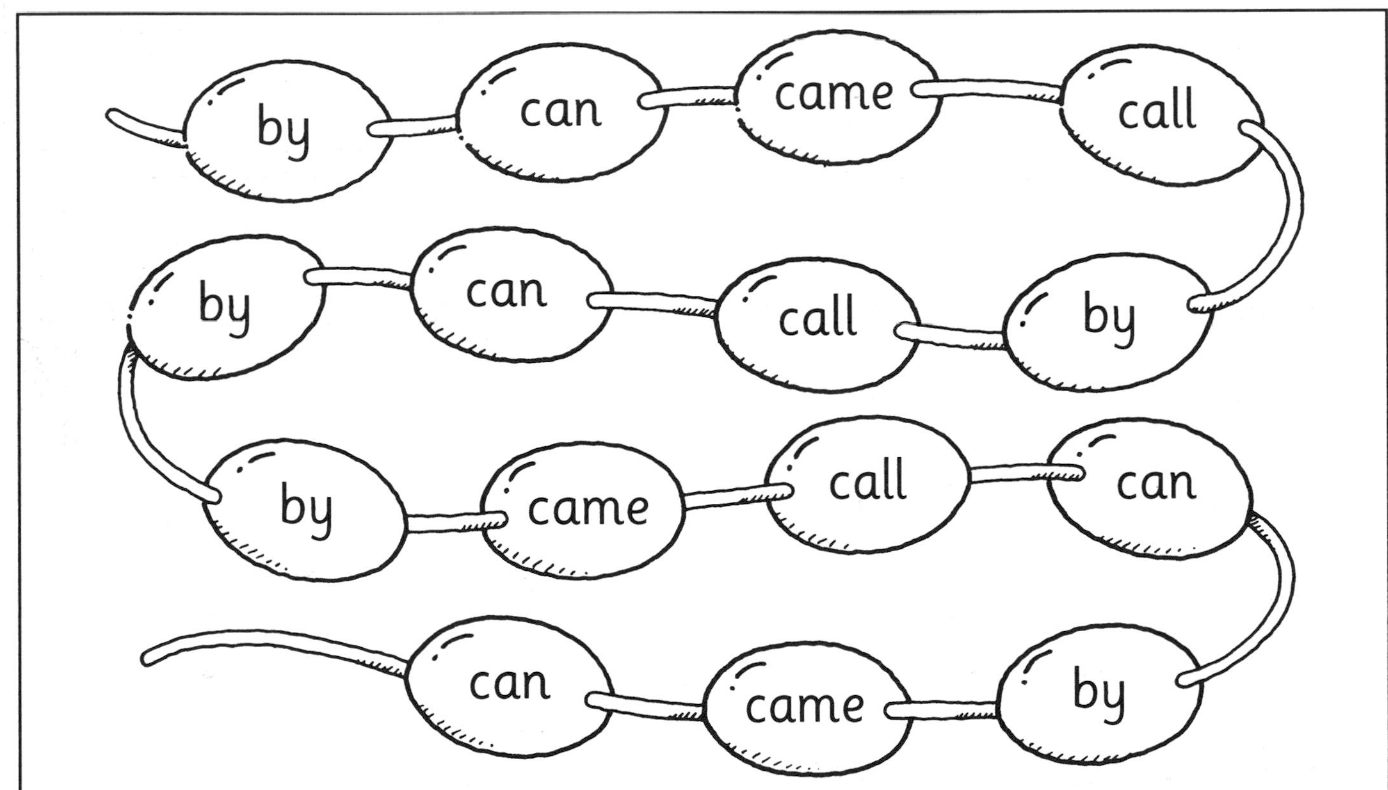

- **Write sentences for these words.**

call   came   can   by

- **Without copying, write these words.**

call   came   can   by

Teachers' note Ask the children to look for these words in the books. They could make a tally of the number of times they find each word.

One, two, three, four, five

• **Read each number word.**

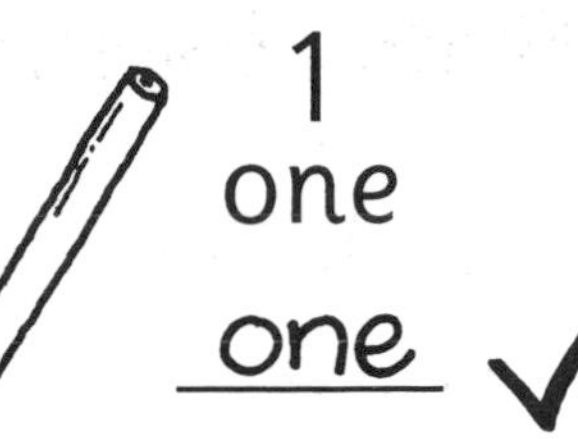

• **Look and say** • **Cover.** • **Write.** • **Check.**

1 one	2 two	3 three	4 four	5 five
6 six	7 seven	8 eight	9 nine	10 ten

• **Read the rhyme.**

• **Write the number words in the spaces.**

One, ________ ,three, ________ , ________ ,

Once I caught a fish alive.

Six, ________ , ________ ,nine, ________ ,

Then I let it go again.

• **Which number rhymes with** alive**?** ________

• **Which number rhymes with** again**?** ________

• **Without copying, write the words for the numbers one to ten.**

• **Write a word which rhymes with each number.**

Teachers' note Copy the rhyme on to a board or large piece of paper to use as a shared text during the whole class introduction. Can the children think of other words which rhyme with each number?

Number match

• Join the partners.

11 12 13 14 15 16 17 18 19 20

twenty eighteen thirteen seventeen twelve fourteen nineteen sixteen eleven fifteen

Now try this!

• Write the numbers from 11 to 20.

• Write these numbers as words.

Teachers' note Ask the children to look at these number words in sets of three, and to Look, Say, Cover, Write and Check them.

Days

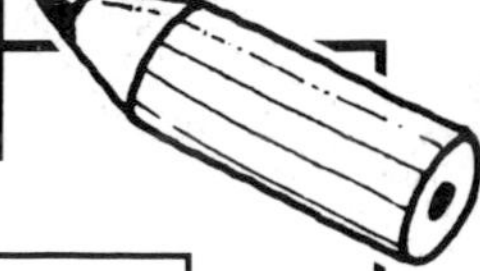

- **Read the words in the box.**
- **Complete these words.**

Days of the week
Monday
Tuesday
Wednesday
Thursday
Friday
Saturday
Sunday

S _ _ _ _ day

S _ _ _ _ y

- **Find the days and circle them.**
- **List them.**

T	h	u	r	s	d	a	y	F	o	r
d	h	r	s	a	d	a	S	r	m	i
y	u	r	d	s	s	t	u	i	d	a
t	y	a	d	d	M	o	n	d	a	y
d	d	S	a	t	u	r	d	a	y	d
W	e	d	n	e	s	d	a	y	o	o
T	u	e	s	d	a	y	y	a	e	b

- **Turn over this page.**
- **Without copying, write the names of the days.**

Teachers' note Provide a collection of diaries and calendars. Encourage the children to read the names of the days of the week in different text styles and layouts.

Sneeze on Monday

Monday Tuesday Wednesday Thursday Friday Saturday Sunday

- **Read the rhyme.**

Sneeze on Monday, sneeze for danger.
Sneeze on Tuesday, meet a stranger.
Sneeze on Wednesday, get a letter.
Sneeze on Thursday, something better.
Sneeze on Friday, sneeze for sorrow.
Sneeze on Saturday, see your friends tomorrow.

- **Write the days of the week.**

____________________ ____________________

____________________ ____________________

____________________ ____________________

____

- **With a friend, make up a new** 'Sneeze on Monday' **rhyme.**
- **These words may help.**

sweet money tonight honey a fright neat

Teachers' note Copy the rhyme on to a board or a large piece of paper to use as a shared text during the whole class introduction. Introduce the new words which could be used to replace the rhyming words at the end of each line.

Family word bank

• **Draw lines to show who they are.**

grandmother	grandfather

sister	brother	mother	father

• **Who are they? Write in the boxes.**

• **List four more family names.**

Teachers' note The activity could be introduced with a shared text which features members of a family. Ask the children to point out the family words.

Cars and roads

- Join a car from each road to make a word.
- Say the word.
- Write the word.

men ______ ______ ______ ______

- Make other words using the cars, in any order.

Now try this!

______ ______ ______ ______

______ ______ ______ ______

______ ______ ______ ______

Teachers' note To provide more practice, mask the letters on the cars before copying them and write other letters in their place. During the extension activity the children can use any letter from the top, then the middle, then the bottom line.

Beginning sounds 

- **Read the words.**
- **Circle their beginning sounds.**
- **Copy the words on to the pictures.**

beads	jewels	sand	beans
jelly	soap	salt	butter
potatoes	pins	pickles	jam

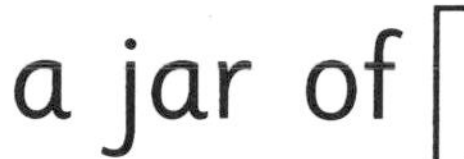

a sack of s

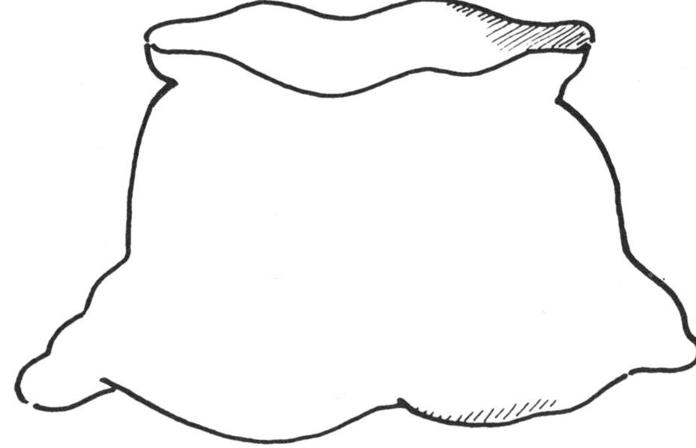

a pan of p

Now try this!

a glass of 

- **Write three words in each picture.**

Teachers' note During the plenary session, the children could play a verbal game in which they add anything they like, however silly, to the containers, for example, 'In my jar I have jelly, jam, jewels, James, a jaguar...'.

Beginning sounds c d t v

- **Read the words.**
- **Circle their beginning sounds.**
- **Copy the words on to the pictures.**

corn	tea	dust	candy
gold	dates	dice	grapes
toffee	cake	grain	toast

a crate of c

a dish of d

a glass of g

a tin of t

- **Draw a picture of these.**

  a heap of h   a spoon of s.

- **Write three words in each picture.**

Teachers' note During the plenary session, the children could play a verbal game in which they add anything they like, however silly, to the containers, for example, 'In the crate there is some corn, Claire, a cake, some cornflakes, a cat...'.

Word endings at et ot

- Make words from the beginnings and endings.
- Read the words.

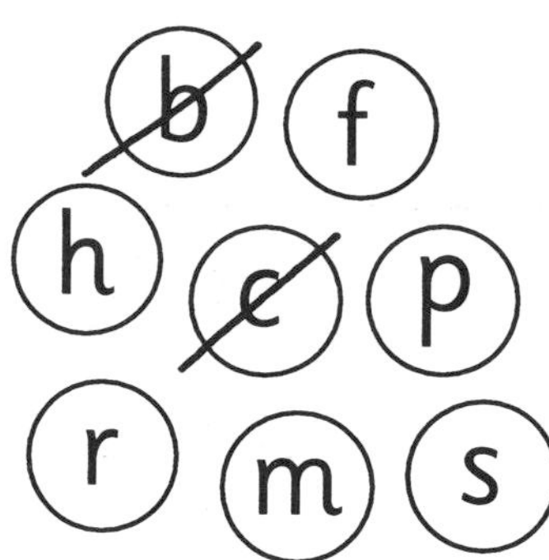

bat ______

cat ______

______ ______

______ ______

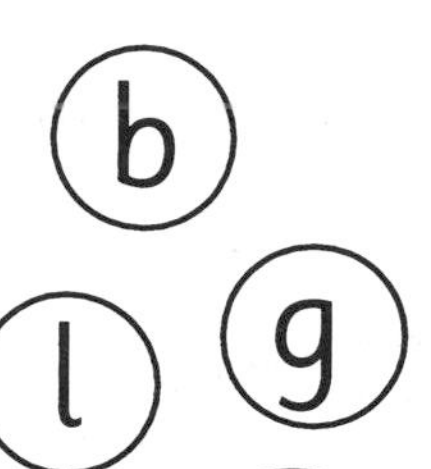

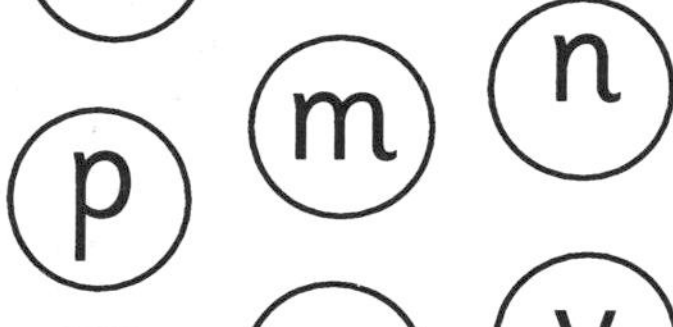

______ ______

______ ______

______ ______

______ ______

______ ______

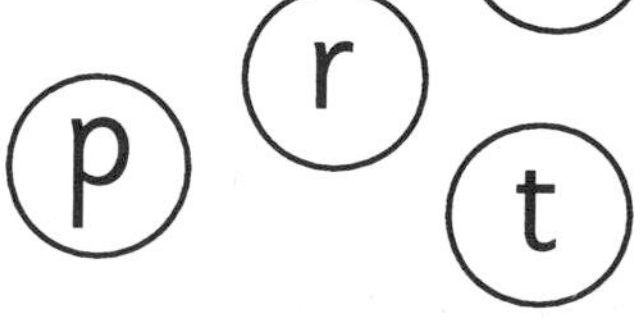

______ ______

______ ______

______ ______

______ ______

______

- Write three silly sentences like this with the rhyming words you have made.

A vet met a wet pet.

Teachers' note The beginnings and endings could be masked and replaced with others of your choice, for example, endings **it**, **im**, **em**, **am**.

Word endings an en in

- Make words from the beginnings and endings.
- Read the words.

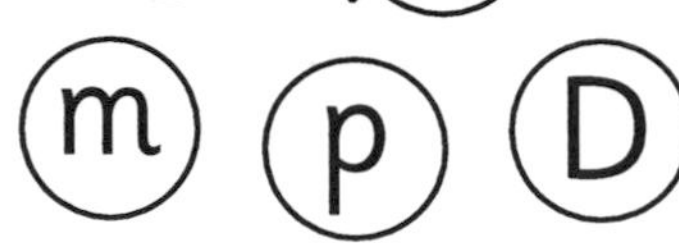

can ________

fan ________

________ ________

____

B d h K p m t

Ben ________

________ ________

________ ________

____

b d f p s t w

________ ________

________ ________

________ ________

____

- Write three silly sentences like this with the rhyming words you have made.

A can man had a tan fan.

Teachers' note The beginnings and endings could be deleted and replaced with others of your choice, for example, endings **ag**, **eg**, **og**.

Word endings ag eg ig

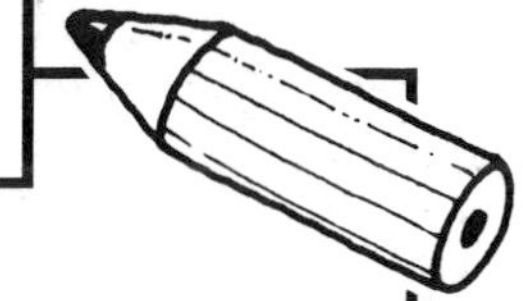

• **Make words from the beginnings and endings.**

• **Read the words.**

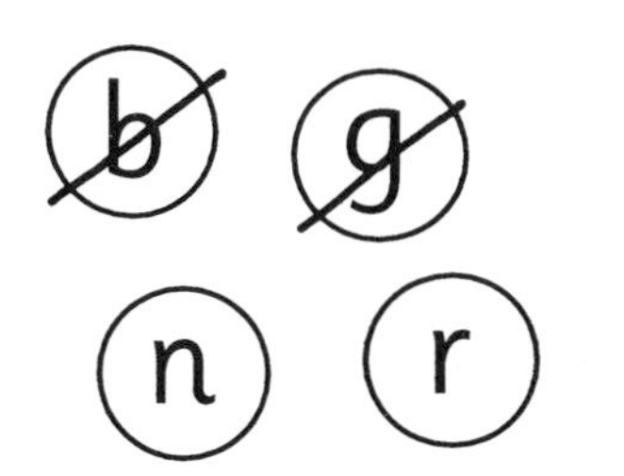

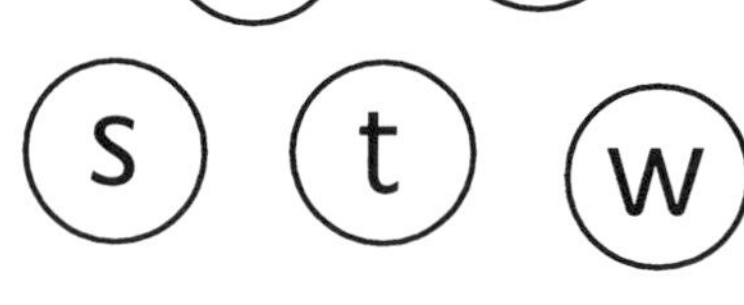

bag ________

gag ________

________ ________

____

---

b M p l

________ ________

____

---

b d f j p w

ig

________ ________

________ ________

________ ________

• **Write three silly sentences like this with the rhyming words you have made.**

A rag is in the bag.

Teachers' note The beginnings and endings could be deleted and replaced with others of your choice, for example, endings **ad**, **od**, **ed**.

Word endings un ug ut

- **Make words from the beginnings and endings.**
- **Read the words.**

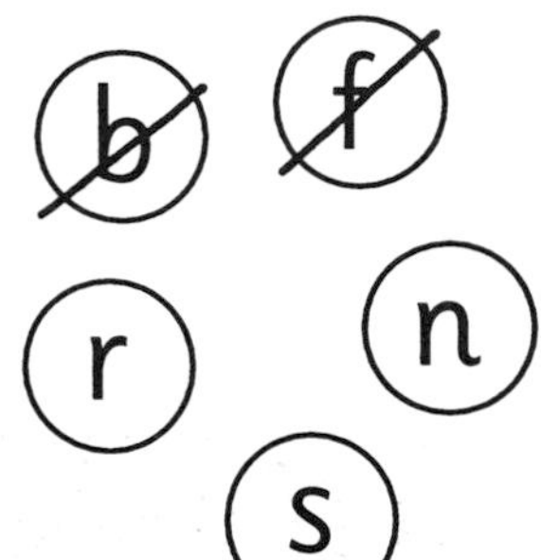

bun ______

fun ______

______

b j h t d r m

______ ______

______ ______

______ ______

______

b c h g n p

______ ______

______ ______

______ ______

- **Write three silly sentences like this with the rhyming words you have made.**

I run in the sun with a bun.

Teachers' note The beginnings and endings could be deleted and replaced with others of your choice, for example, endings **id**, **od**, **ud**.

Making new words 1

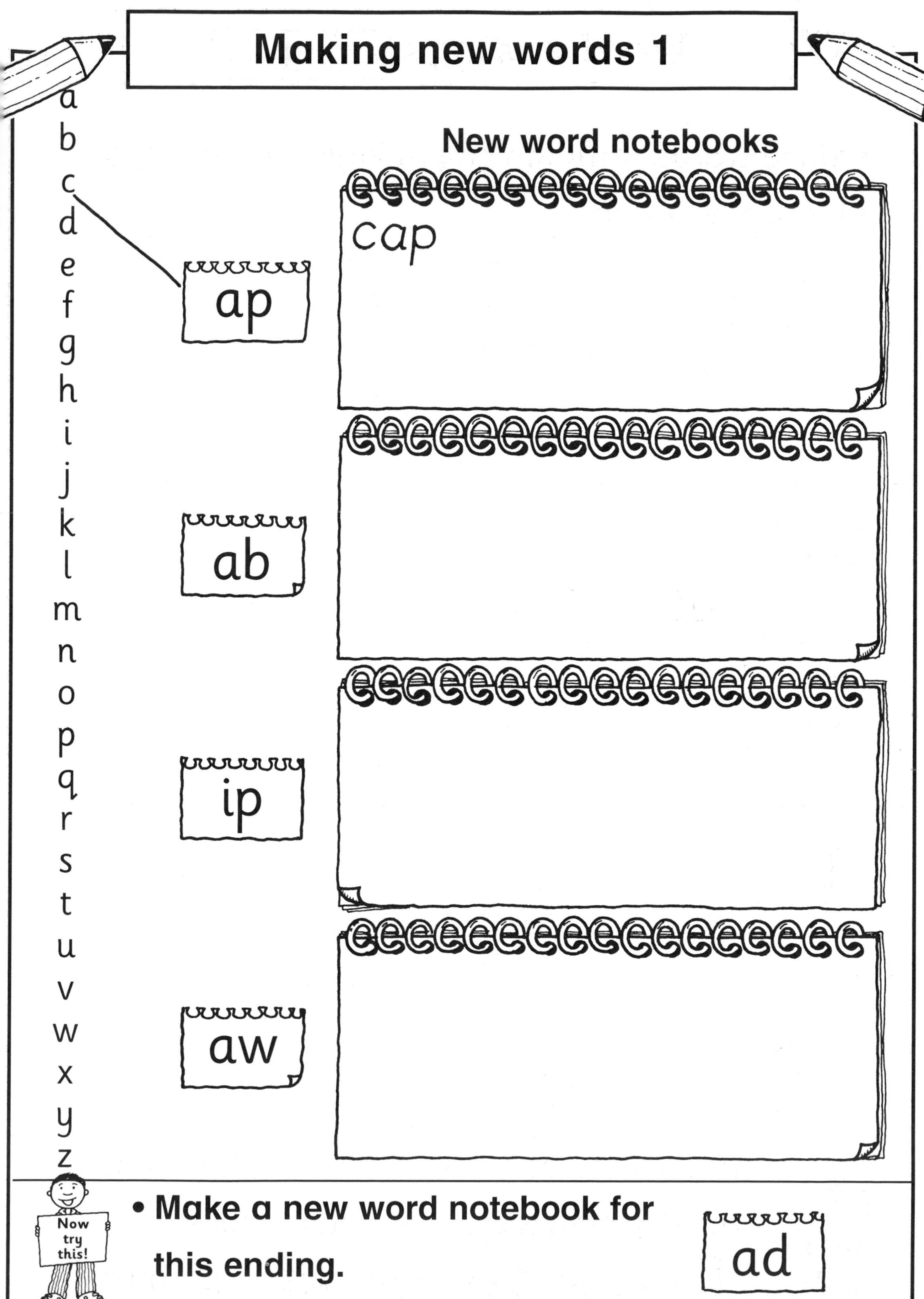

- **Make a new word notebook for this ending.**

ad

Teachers' note The children could share the words they have made. Ask them whether they included the words: bap, sap, gab, lab. Do they know what they mean? Help them to identify the correct spelling of words they spelt wrongly, for example, 'wip'.

Making new words 2

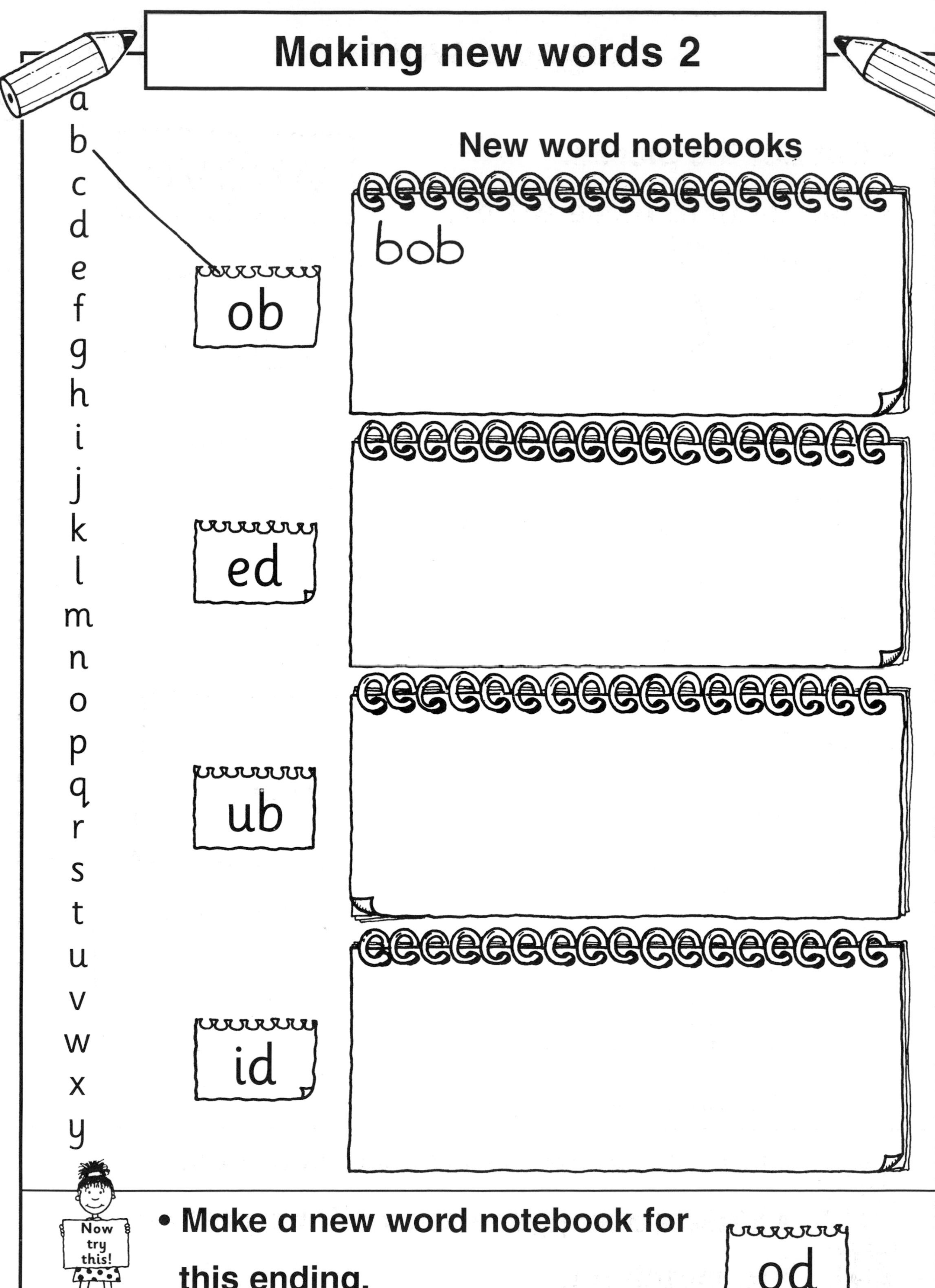

• **Make a new word notebook for this ending.**

od

Teachers' note The children could share the words they have made, Ask them whether they included these words: fob, hob, lob, mob, dub. Do they know what they mean? Help them to identify the correct spelling of words they spelt wrongly, for example, 'ded', 'hed' and 'sed'.

Jigsaw words

• Cut out the pieces.

• Join them to make words.

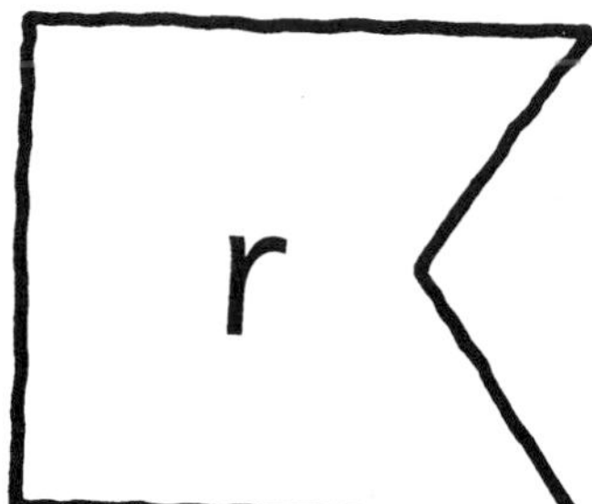

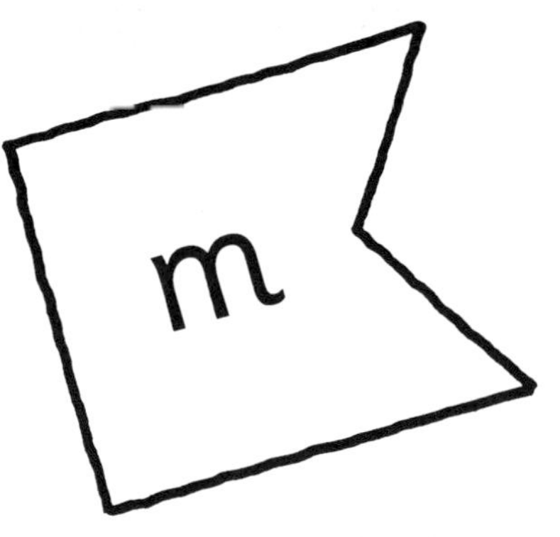

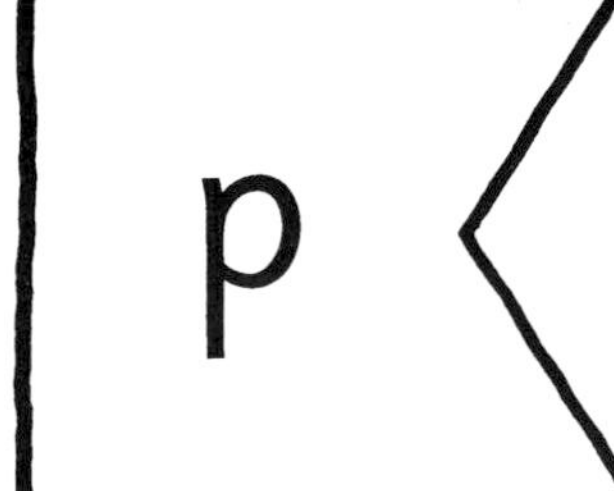

• List all the real words you can make.

• Make some jigsaw words for a partner to match up.

Teachers' note The beginnings and endings could be masked and replaced with others of your choice, such as, beginnings **p,l,b,h**; endings **age, ike, ate** and **ill**.

Word spinner

- Glue this page on to card.
- Cut out the word spinners.
- Use them for the word spinner game.

Beginnings

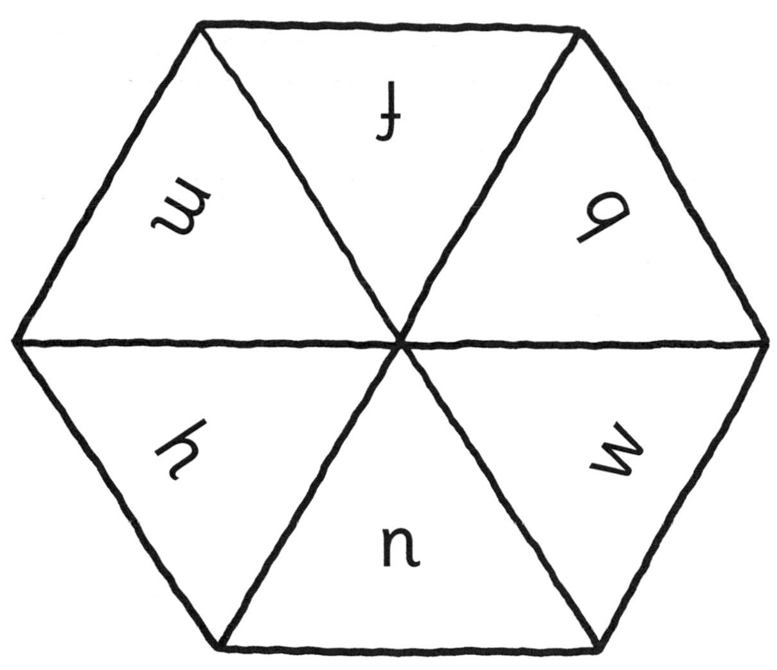

Endings

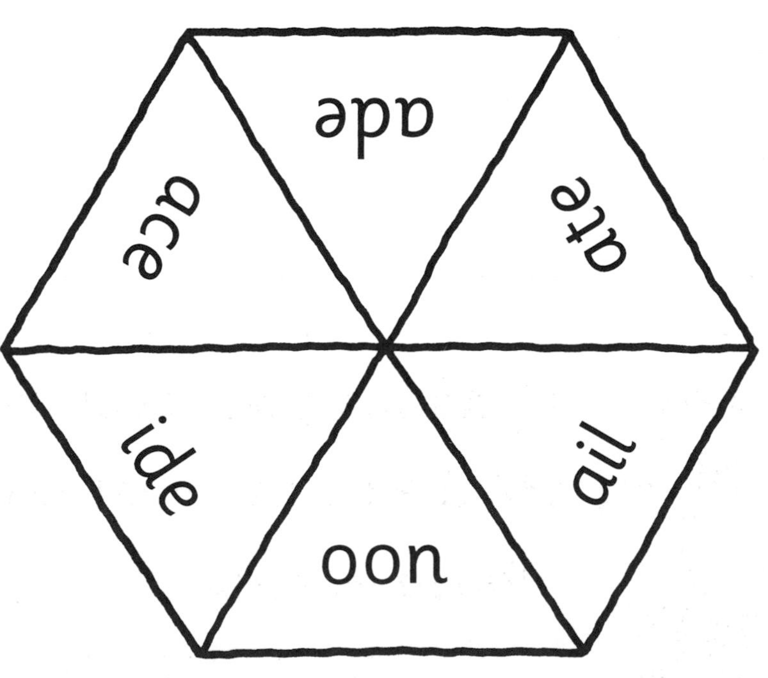

Teachers' note The beginning and endings could be masked and replaced with others of your own choice, such as, beginnings **b,c,d,h,l,s**; endings **one, oat, orn, ent, ong, ang**.

Word spinner game

- Play with a partner. Take turns.
- Spin a beginning.
- Spin an ending.
- List the words on the chart.

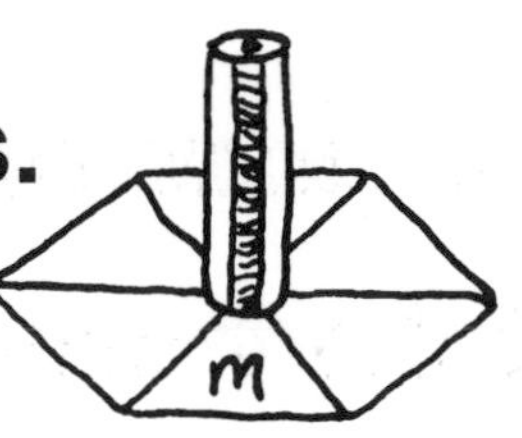

made

Only list real words.

Name ______________	Name ______________

- Choose your own beginning letters.
- Make some other real words with these endings.

ade | ide | ate

Teachers' note The children can use dictionaries to check whether or not the words they have made are 'real' words.

End sounds

- Look at the pictures.
- Say the words.
- Draw a line to join each end sound to a picture.

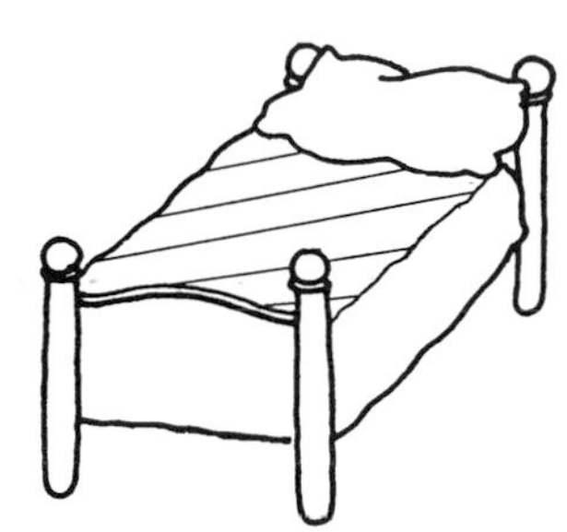

p

t

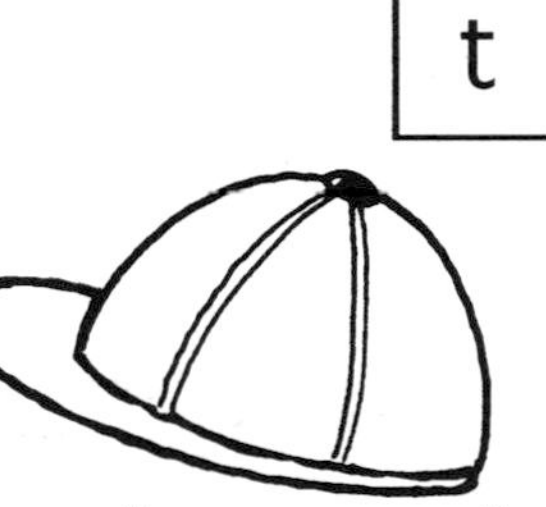

- Write the end sound.

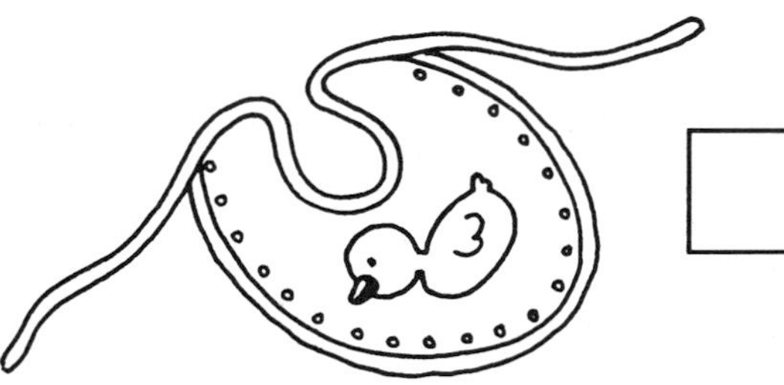

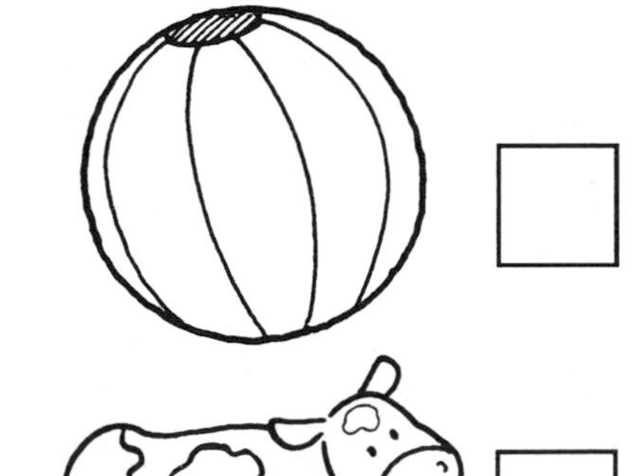

- List four things in your classroom which end in n.

Teachers' note The children could cut pictures from magazines and catalogues, of things which end with letters of your choice, for example, **x, g, d, p, t, n.**

Bees

• **Make** ee **words.**

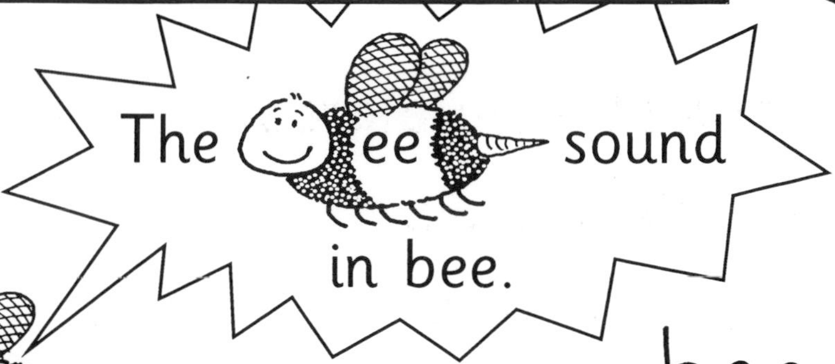

The ee sound
in bee.

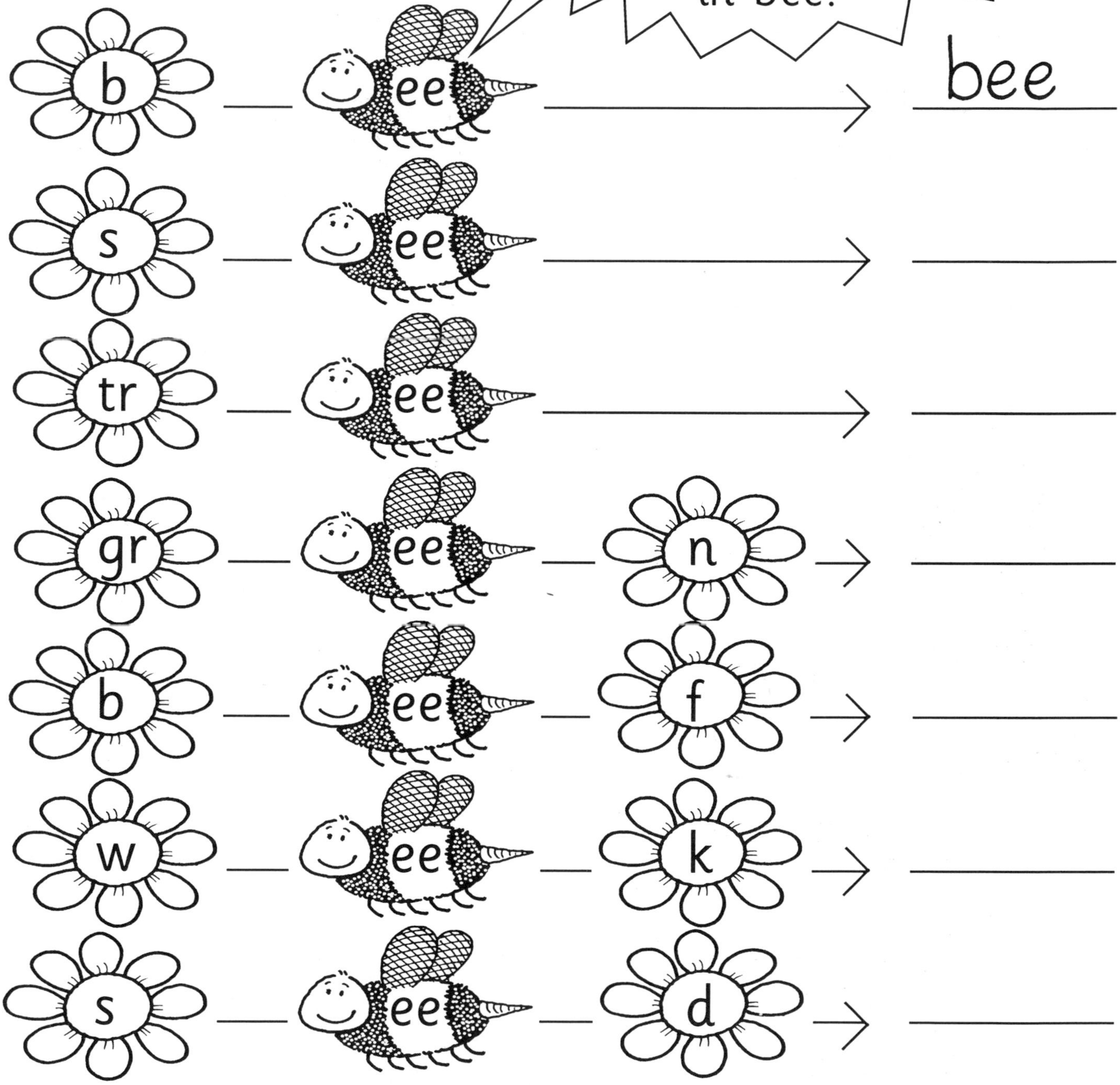

b — ee → bee
s — ee →
tr — ee →
gr — ee — n →
b — ee — f →
w — ee — k →
s — ee — d →

Now
try
this!

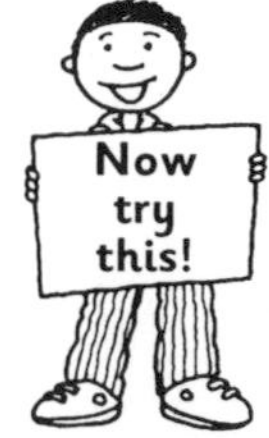

• **Look for** ee **words in books.**

• **List them.**

Teachers' note Introduce the activity with a rhyme or story, as a shared text, which incudes the phoneme **ee**.

Boots

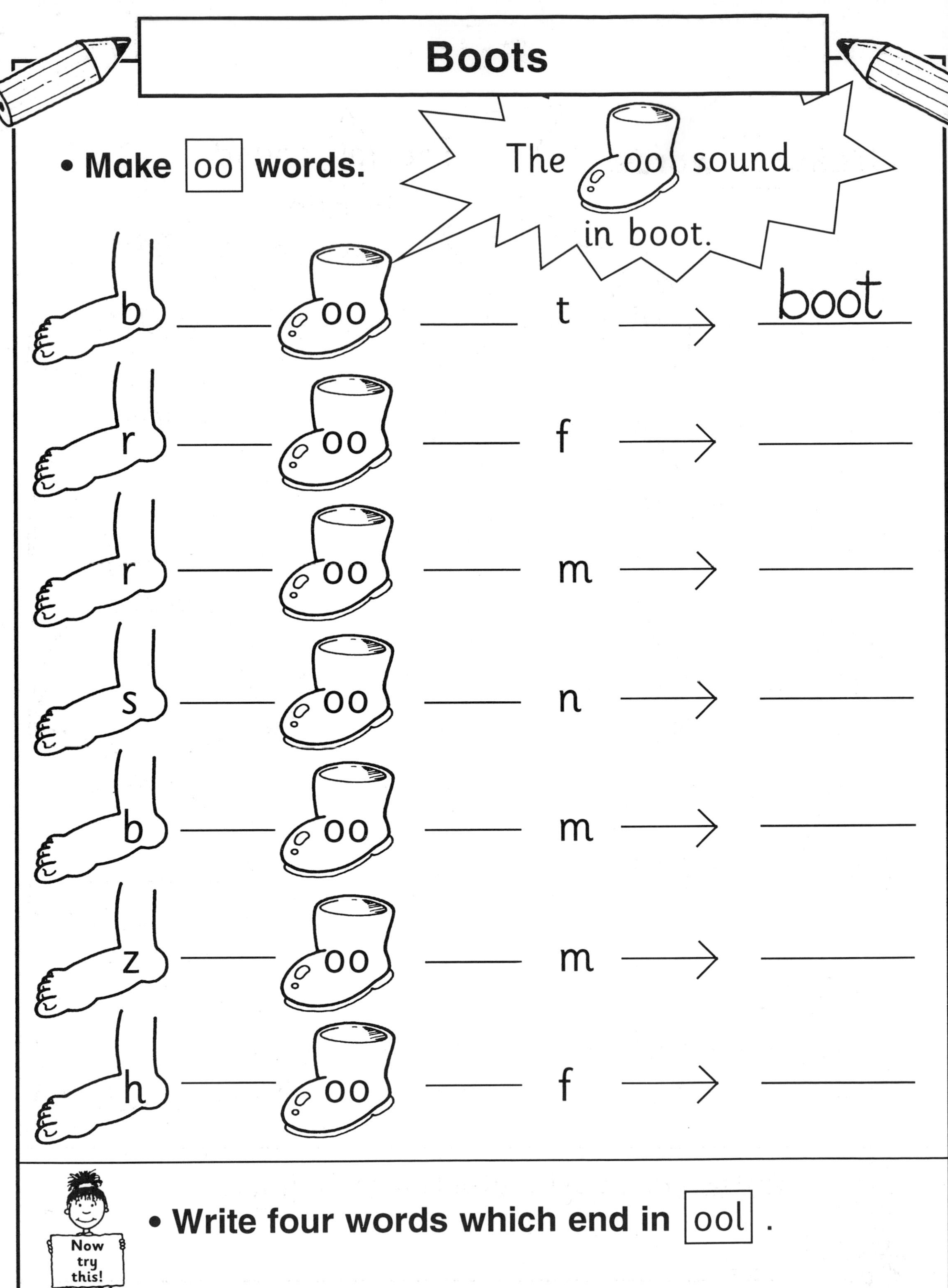

• **Write four words which end in** ool .

Now try this!

Teachers' note Introduce the activity with a rhyme or a story, as a shared text, which includes the phoneme **oo** (long as in boot, not short as in book).

Rain

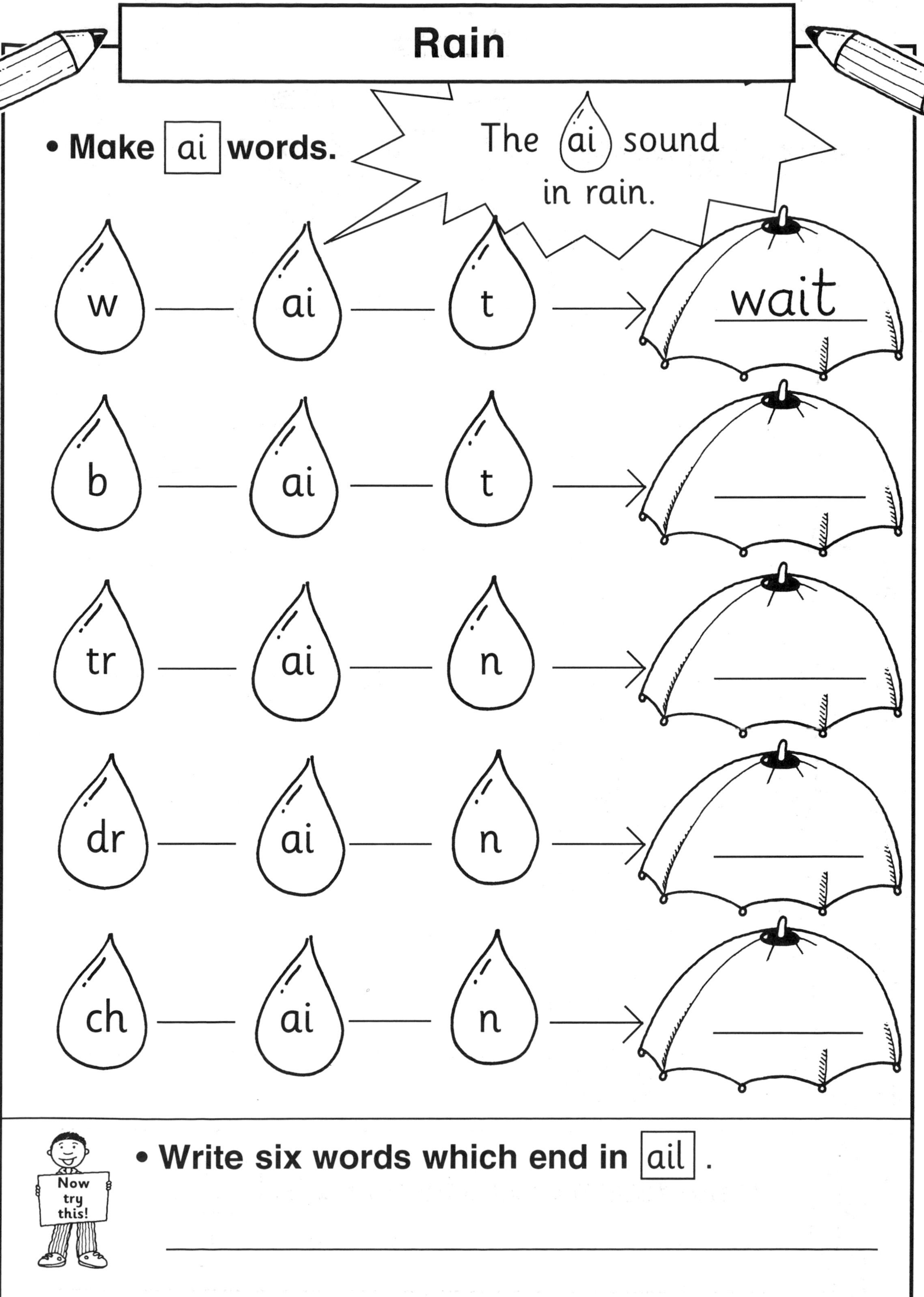

Teachers' note Introduce the activity with a rhyme or story, as a shared text, which includes the phoneme **ai**.

Finding phonemes 1

- Say the words.
- Listen for the same middle sounds.

Draw lines to join them.

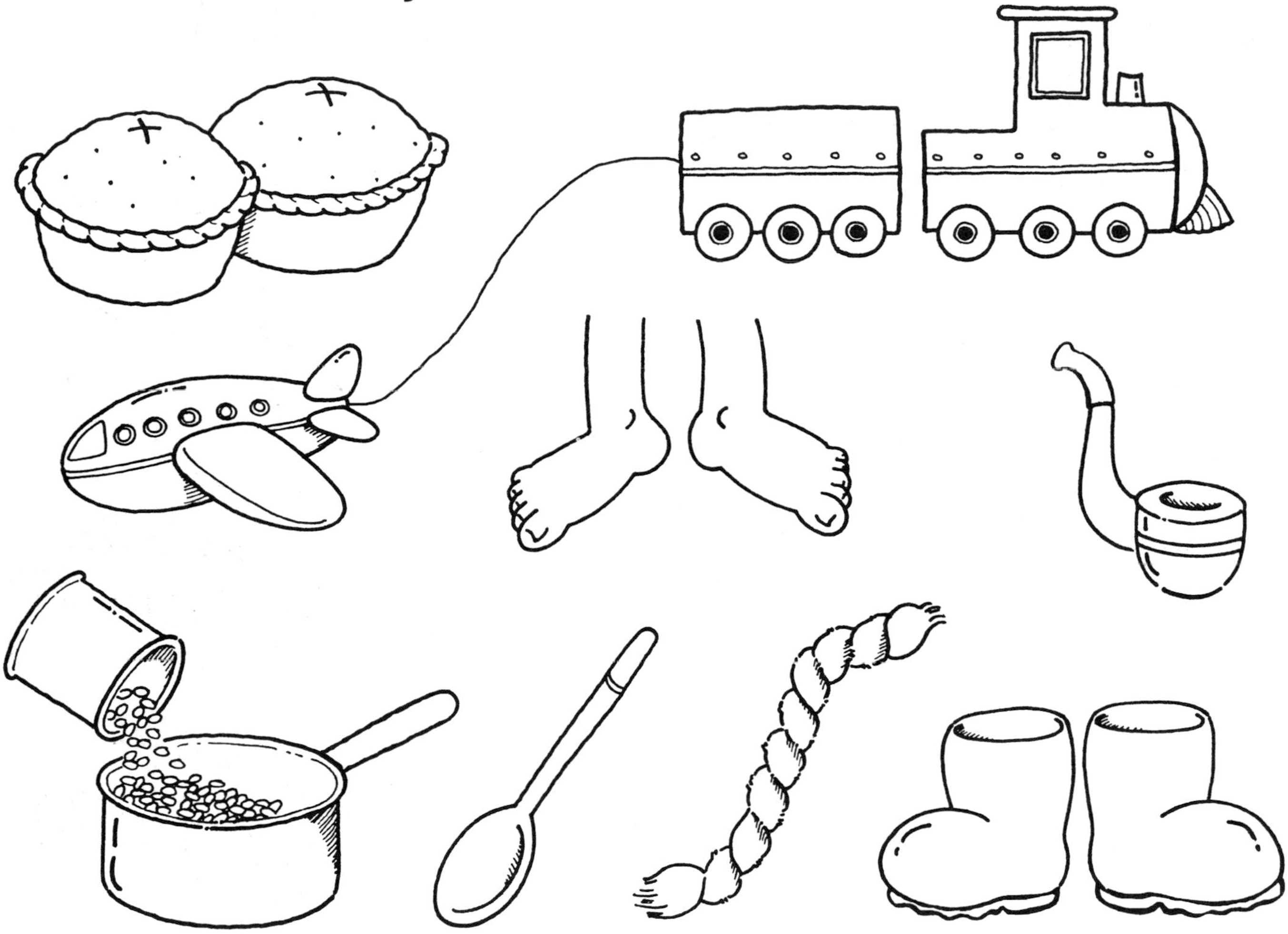

- With a partner, say these words.

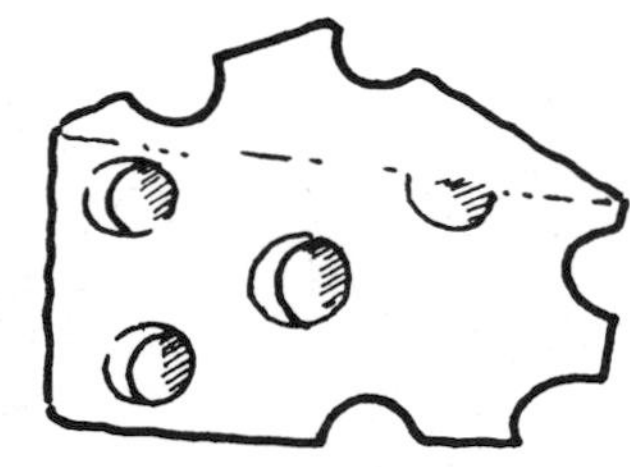

- List four words with the same middle sounds as each of these words.

Teachers' note Introduce the activity with a game in which the children suggest other words which have the same middle phonemes (however they are spelled) as those in the activity. Write them in a table with a column for each phoneme.

Finding phonemes 2

- Say the words.
- Listen for the same middle sounds.

  Draw lines to join them.

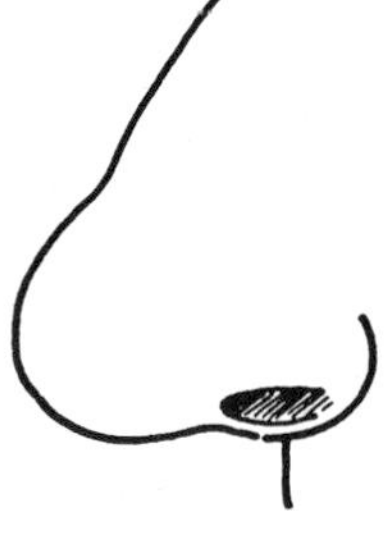

- With a partner, say these words.

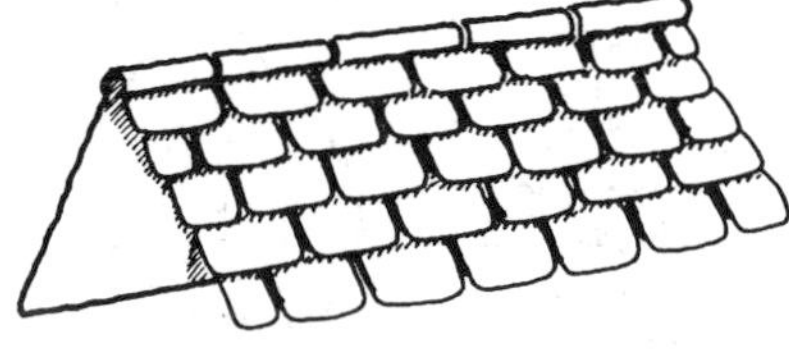

- List four words with the same middle sounds as each of these words.

Teachers' note Introduce the activity with a game in which the children suggest other words which have the same middle phonemes (however they are spelled) as those in the activity. Write them in a table with a column for each phoneme.

Plurals with s

Singular means one.
Plural means more than one.

- **Read the words on the notepad.**
- **Copy them on to the cats' books.**

chairs
books
~~cats~~
pencil
school
pencils
~~cat~~
book
pens
schools
chair
pen

singular
cat

plural
cats

- **Draw lines to match each singular to its plural.**

Teachers' note A whole class introduction could feature a rhyme or song which includes singulars and plurals, such as, *Ten green bottles.* Ask the children to spot the plural words in the rhymes.

y endings

- **Add y to make words.**

m __ cr __ b __ dr __

tr __ fl __ sl __ fr __

- **Complete the sentences with the y words you have made.**

Dad can fry fish.

The fox is ______.

I ______ when I am sad.

That is ______ pen.

The chair is ______ the table.

The sun will ______ the washing.

I ______ to be good.

Birds ______.

- **Turn over the page and write the y words you have made.**
- **Read them.**

Teachers' note The rhyme *There was an old woman who swallowed a fly* could be used to show different spellings of the same sound, with the words fly, die and why.

Name wall

- Write a name on the wall.
- Write a word which starts with each letter.

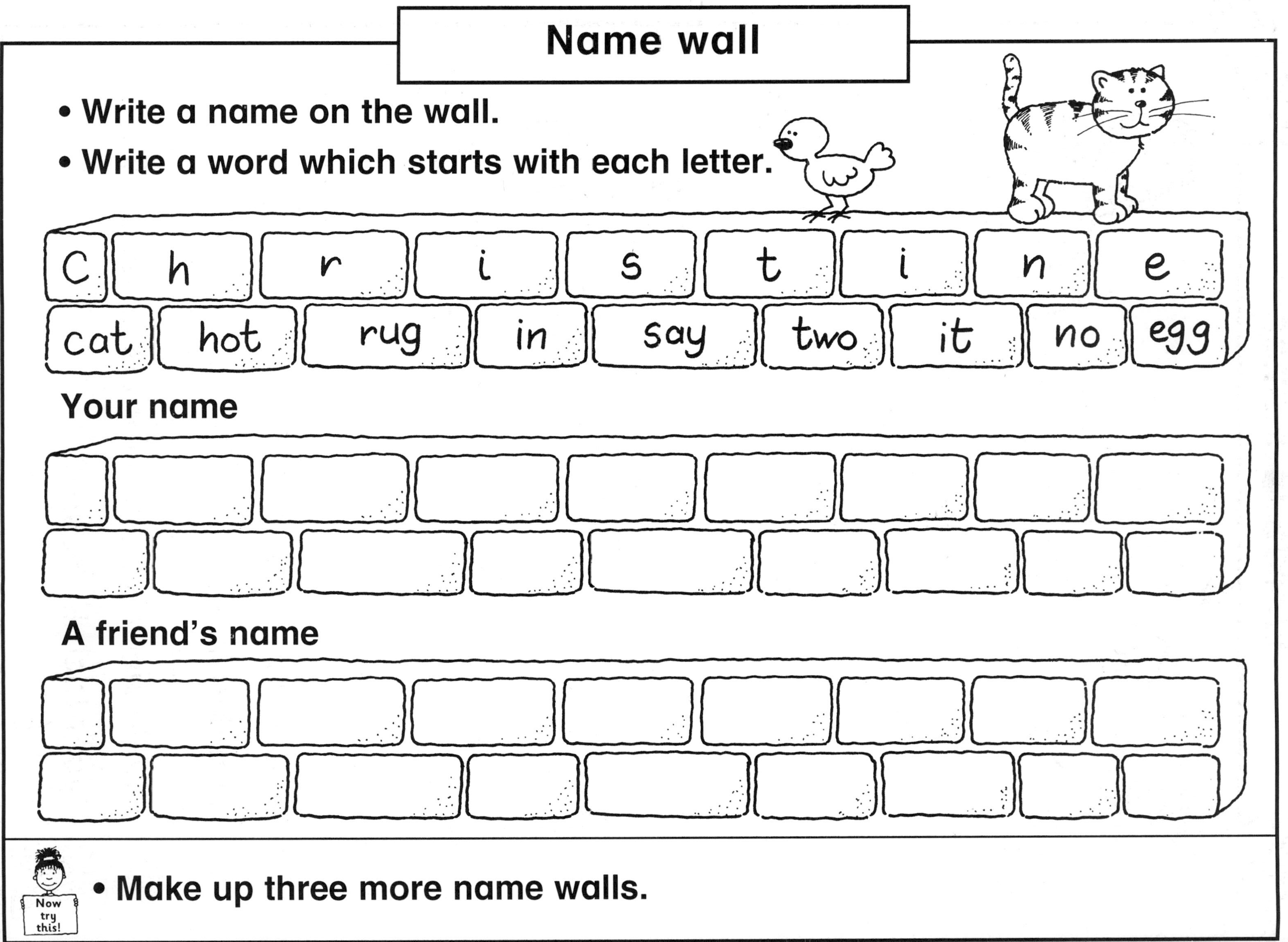

Your name

A friend's name

- Make up three more name walls.

Teachers' note Ensure that the children have started the

Words in names

William ill ran Rani

• Join the children to the right balloons.

man are lot bar jam sun ray

James Barbara Sunil Raymond Gareth Amanda Charlotte

• Write another name.

• Write any small words you can find in it.

• Make word balloons for the small words in your friends' names.

Teachers' note The children could contribute to a display with self-portraits, under which their names are written, together with any words they can find in their names. If their first names can not be used, they could try their middle or family names.

Rhyme trees

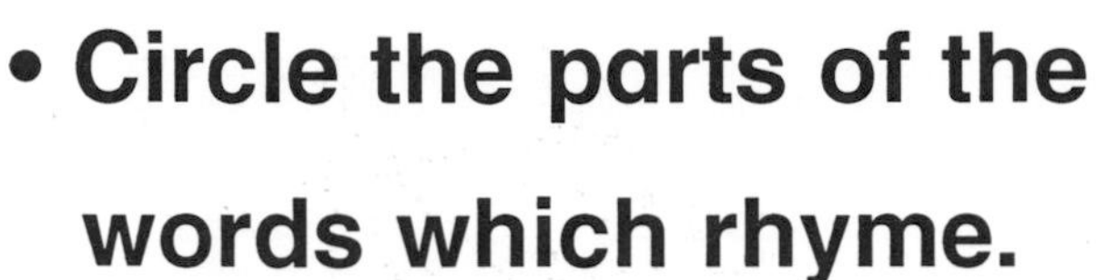

- Circle the parts of the words which rhyme.
- Write the rhyme sound on the empty leaf

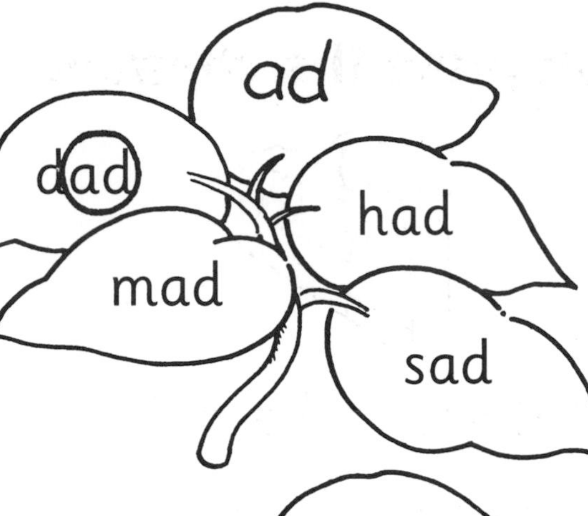

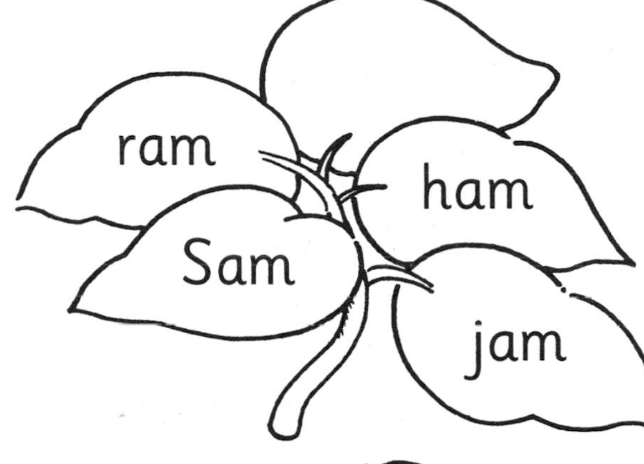

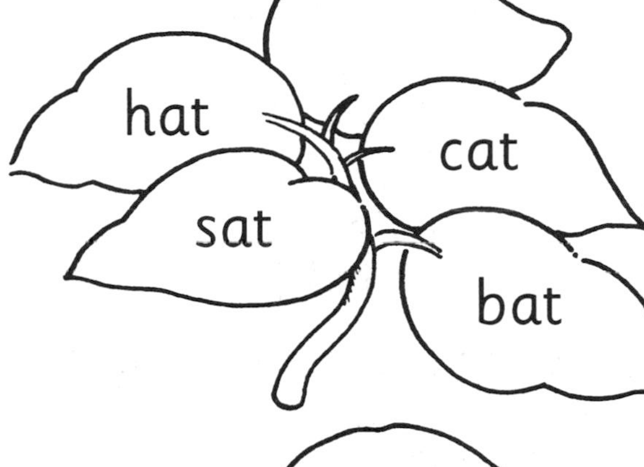

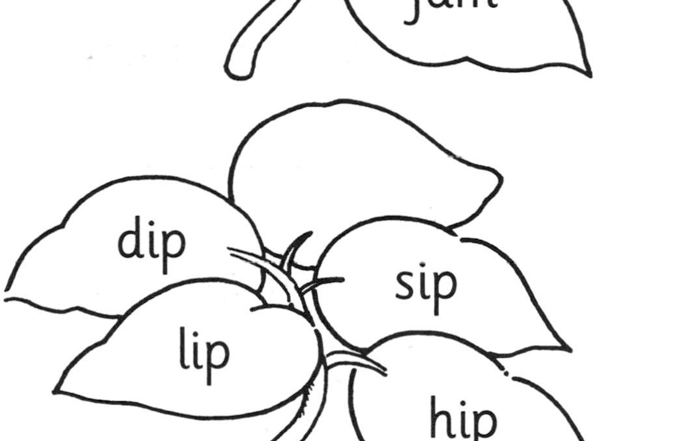

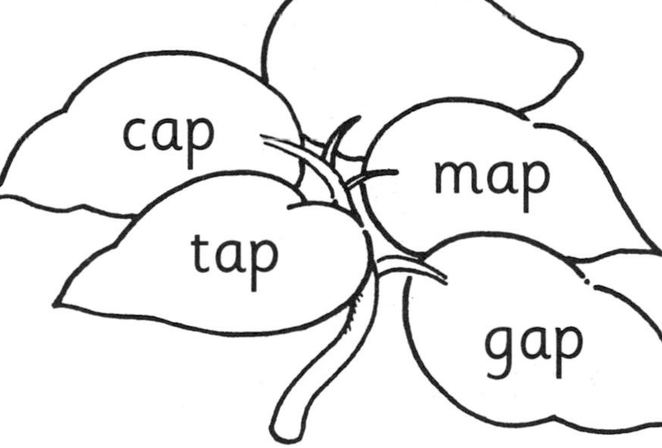

- Fill in these rhyme trees.

- Make two of your own rhyme trees.

Teachers' note Encourage the children to read the rhyming sounds with a partner; one of them can read while the other listens, so that they can check any mistakes.

Make a rhyme

• **Complete the rhymes.**

Where is the ball ?

On the wall.

Where is Fred ?

Under the ________.

Where is the sock ?

On the ________.

Where are the mice ?

On the ________.

Where is the ________?

In the ________.

Where is the car ?

On the ________.

Where is the ________?

In the ________.

• **Write three more rhymes.**

Teachers' note Introduce the activity by reading various nursery rhymes to the children and asking them to identify words which rhyme.

Rhyme time

- **With a partner, find the rhyming words.**
- **Write them in the pictures.**
- **Finish the last rhyme.**

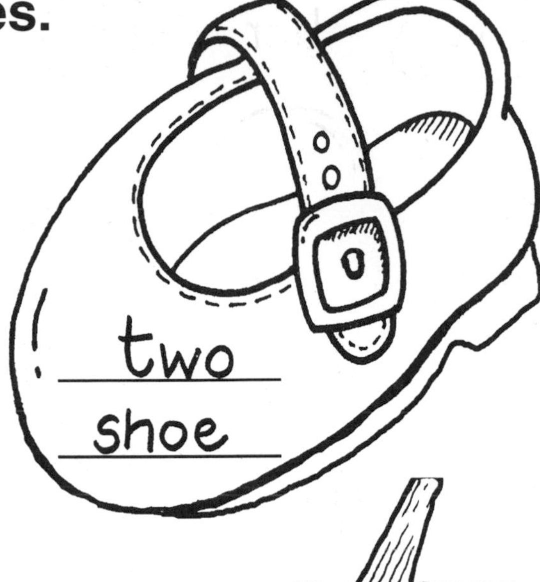

One, two,
Buckle my shoe.

Three, four,
Knock at the door.

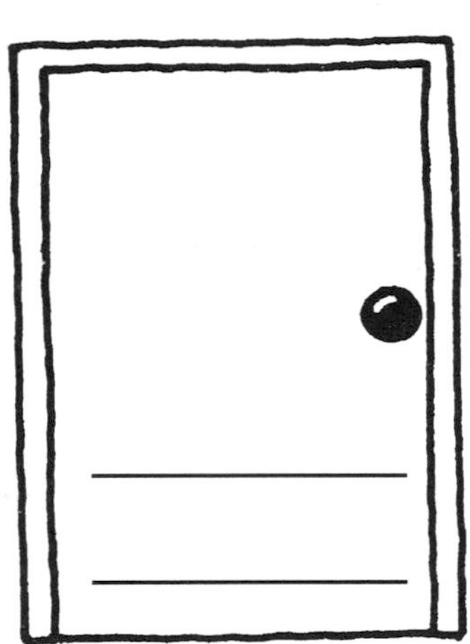

Five, six,
Pick up sticks.

Seven, eight,
Open the gate.

Nine, ten,

________________________.

- **Write other words which rhyme with these numbers.**

two glue
four ______
six ______
eight ______
ten ______

Teachers' note Introduce the activity by using the rhyme as a shared text. Ask the children to think of other words which rhyme with each number. Make a table with a column for each number. The children should notice that rhyming words are not always spelt the same.

Find the rhyme

- **Colour things which rhyme with these words.**

fell - red　　bar - blue　　jail - green　　soon - yellow

- **Complete in the rhyme chart.**

fell	bar	jail	soon
	jar		

- **Write some more words which rhyme with these.**

fell	bar	jail	soon
tell			

Teachers' note During the plenary session, the children could play 'rhyme rounds'. One says a short word, and the others take turns to say another word which rhymes with it. The rhyming words could be used to make silly rhymes.

Ba ll oons

- Complete the words with ll .
- Read the words to a partner.

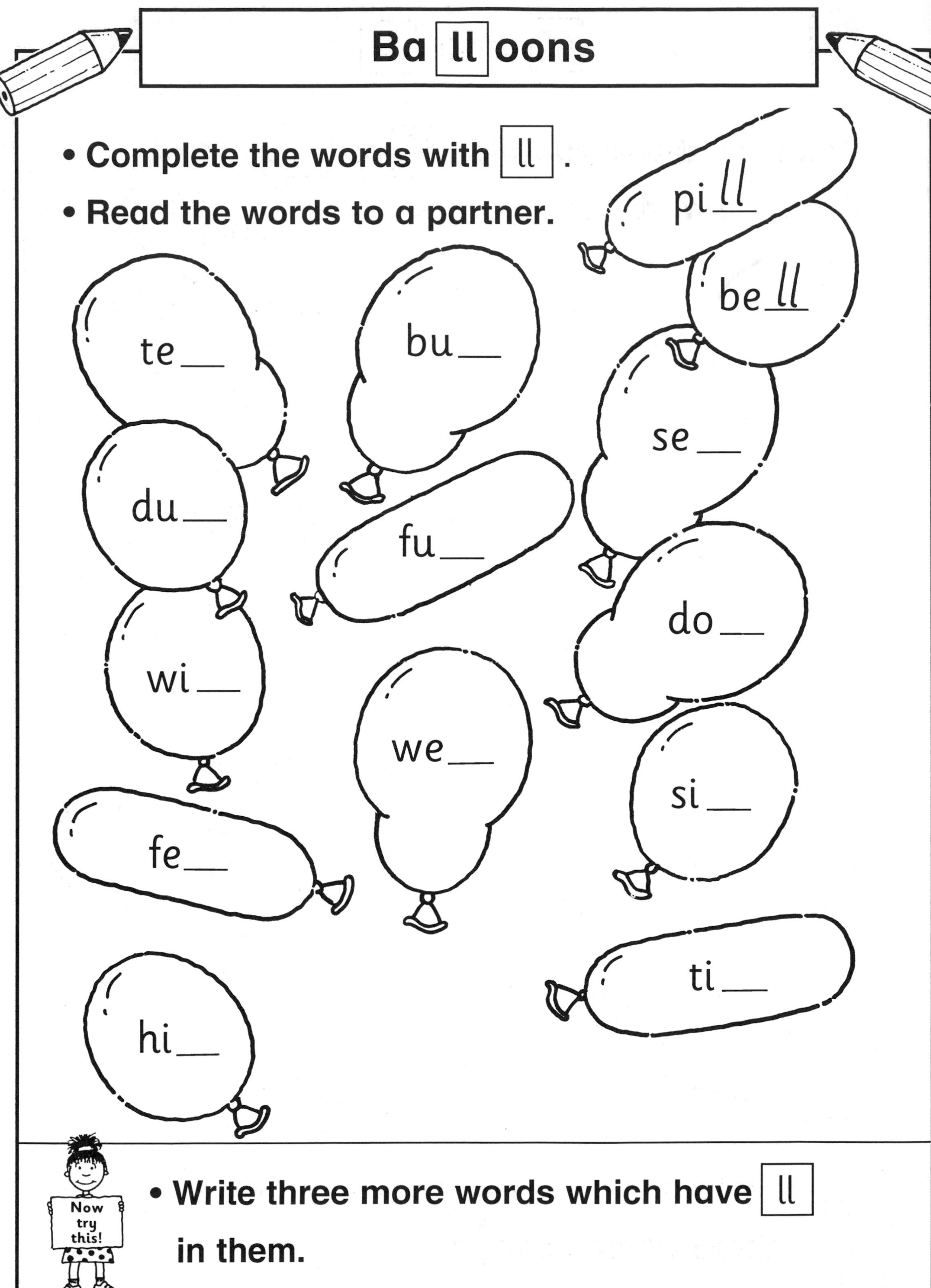

- Write three more words which have ll in them.

Teachers' note Introduce the activity with a rhyme which features double consonants, for example, *Jack and Jill* or *Ding, Dong, Bell*. Ask the children to think of other words which end in ll. Write the words on the board.

ff and ss

- **Complete the words with ff or ss.**
- **Read the words to a partner.**

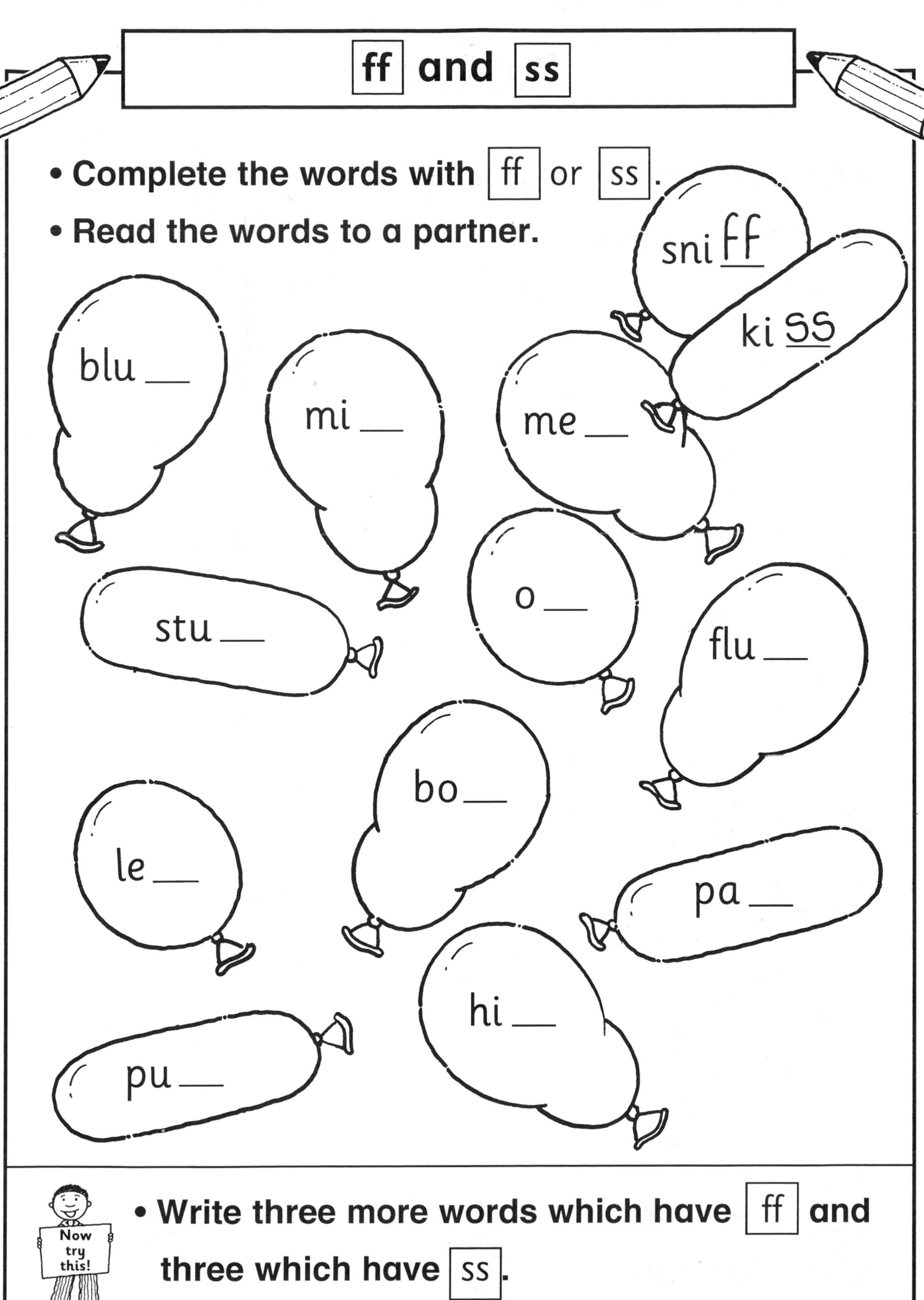

- **Write three more words which have ff and three which have ss.**

Teachers' note During the plenary session invite the children to share the words they found which have **ff** and **ss**. Help them to identify any mistakes, such as 'coff', while acknowledging that the children have correctly identified the sound.

ck

- **Read the words.**
- **Circle** (ck) .

back neck tick sock luck

- **Complete the words.**

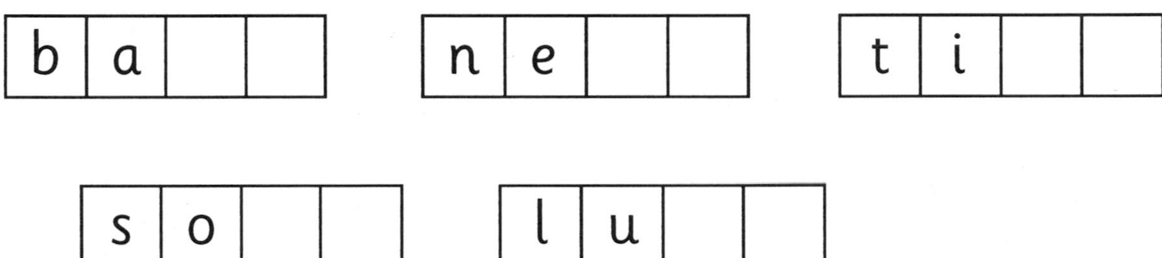

b	a		

n	e		

t	i		

s	o		

l	u		

- **Find the words in the wordsearch.**
- **Colour them yellow.**

l	u	c	k	e	h	b
h	e	a	n	t	s	a
a	t	k	t	h	o	c
t	i	c	k	p	c	k
a	e	n	e	c	k	k

back
neck
tick
sock
luck

- **List six more** ck **words.**
- **The rhyme** 'One, two, buckle my shoe' **may help.**

Teachers' note During the plenary session invite the children to share the words they have found which have **ck**. Write them onto a chart, in columns of rhyming words, such as, back, hack, Jack; lick, pick, trick.

Ding,dong,bell

- **Read the rhyme.**
- **Circle (ng).**

Ding, Dong, bell,
Pussy's in the well.
Who put her in?
Little Johnny Thin.
Who pulled her out?
Little Tommy Stout.

What a naughty boy was that
To try and drown poor pussy cat,
Who never did him harm,
And killed all the mice in his father's barn.
Ding, dong, bell.
Ding, dong, bell.

- **List six more words with ng .**

Teachers' note Copy the rhyme onto a large piece of paper to use, during the introduction, as a shared text. Ask the children to look and listen for words with **ng**. Ask them to think of more of these words, and write them in rhyming lists, for example, bring, sing, king; song, wrong, long.

b and b clusters

- **Say what is in the picture**
- **Complete the words with b, bl or br.**

 __ eak	 __ eads	 __ eetle	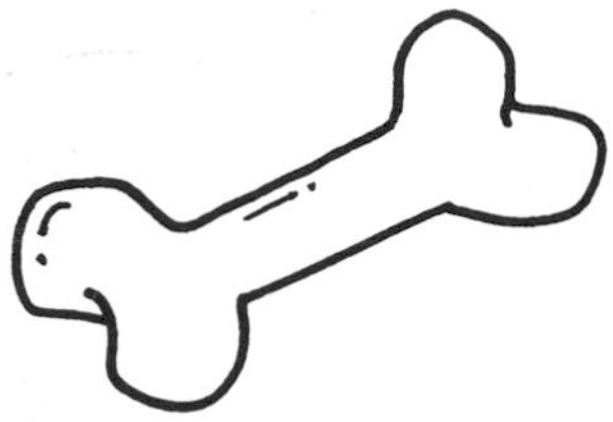 __ one
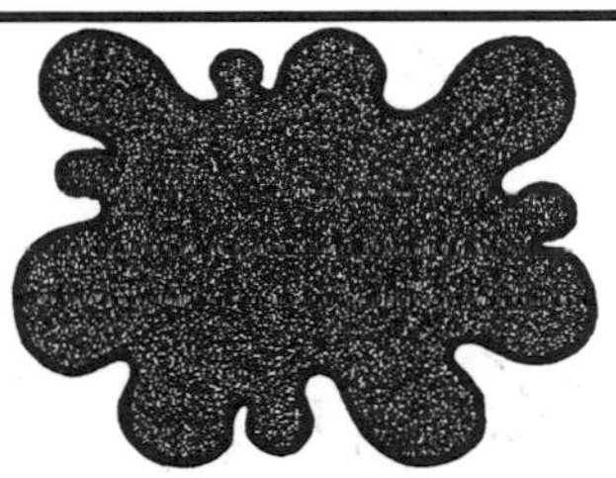 __ __ ack	 __ __ ow	 __ __ ade	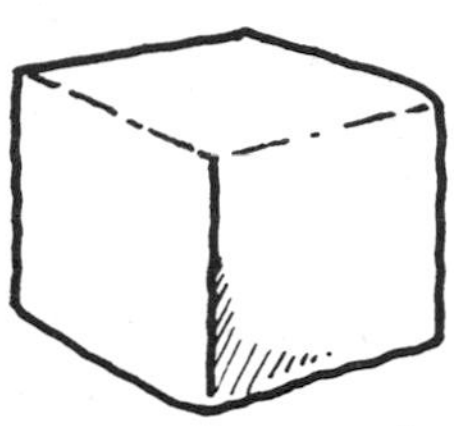 __ __ ock
 __ __ ush	 __ __ ide	 __ __ ead	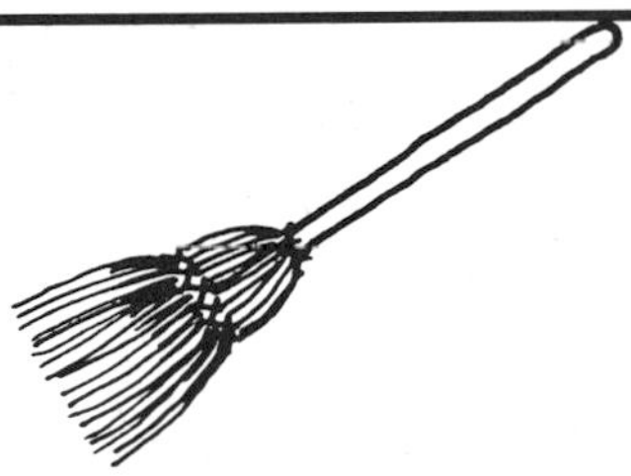 __ __ oom

- **Complete these colours with bl or br.**

__ __ ack __ __ own __ __ ue

- **List six things in your classroom which start with b.**

Teachers' note Introduce the activity with a shared text including **b** words, for example, *Bye baby bunting.* Ask the children to listen for words which begin with **b**. They could think of more of them and then sort them into **bl**, **br** and **b** words.

c and c clusters

- **Colour things beginning with**

cl - blue   cr - red   c - green.

- **List all of the things which begin with cl, cr, c.**

- **Cut out and collect pictures to make a cl page, a cr page and a c page.**

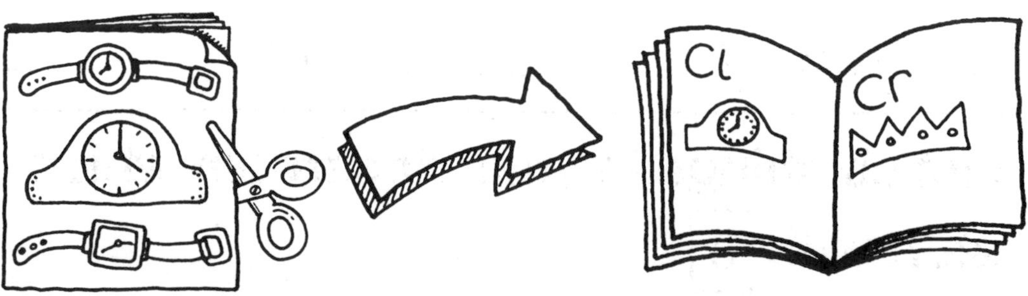

Teachers' note Introduce the activity with a shared text including **c** words, for example, *The Crooked Man**. Ask the children to listen for words which begin with **c**. They could suggest more **c** words and sort them into **cl, cr** and **c** words.

f and f clusters

- **Colour things beginning with**

fr - blue   fl - red   f - green

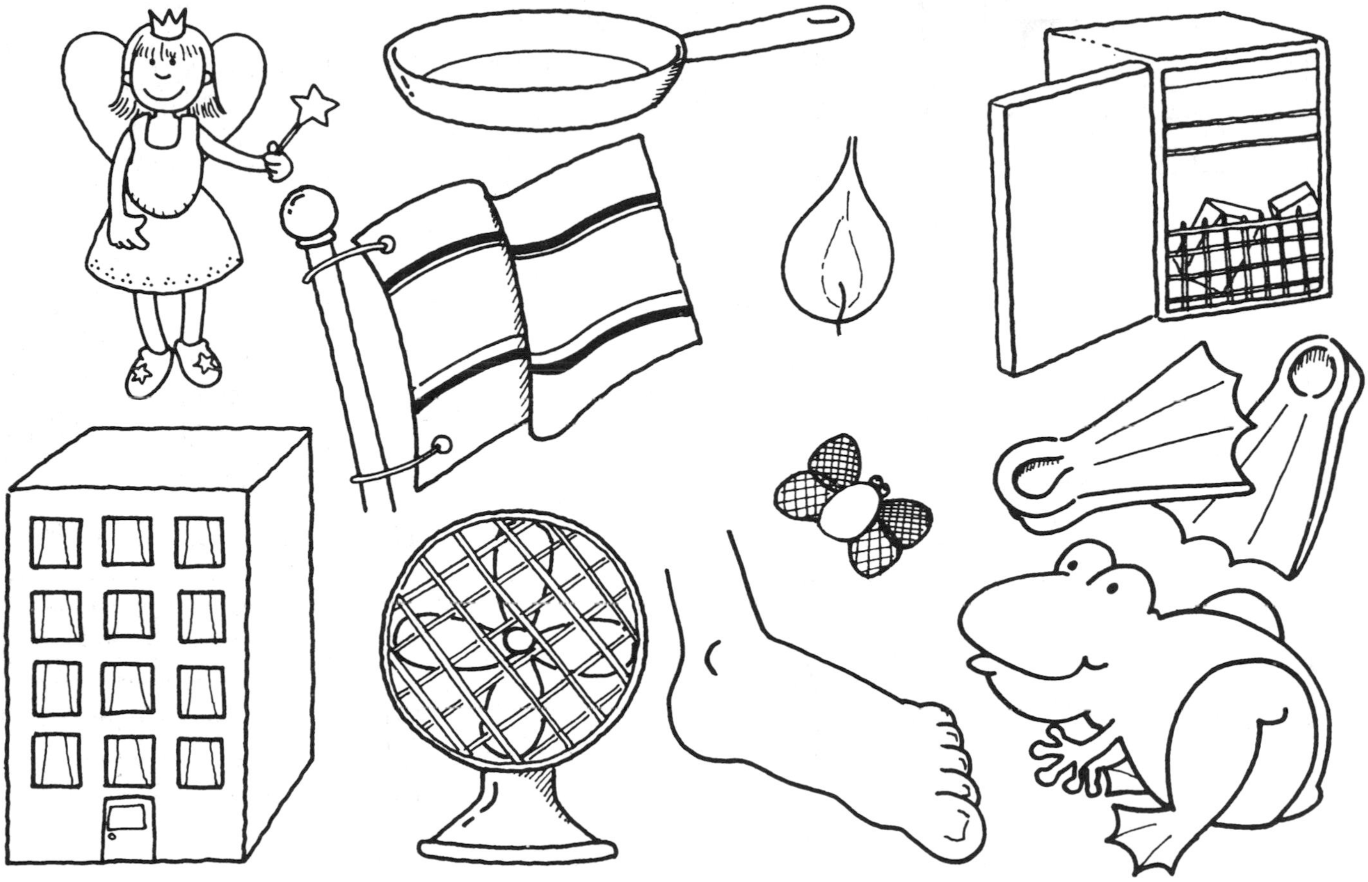

- **List all of the things which begin with fr, fl, f.**

- **Cut out and collect pictures to make a fr page, a fl page and a f page.**

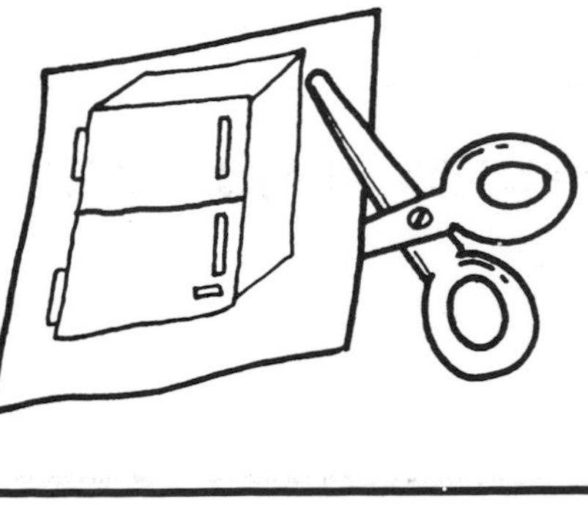

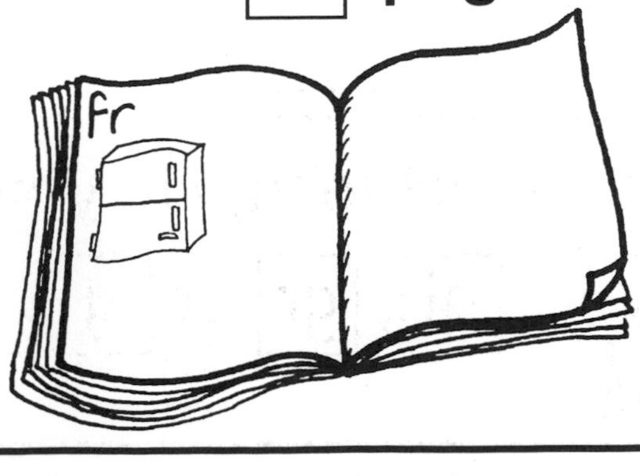

Teachers' note Introduce the activity with a shared text including initial **f** sounds, such as, *My Father was a Frenchman**. Ask the children to listen for words which begin with **f**. They could suggest more and then sort them into **fr, fl** and **f** words.

g and g clusters

- Say what is in the picture.
- Complete the words with gl, gr or g.

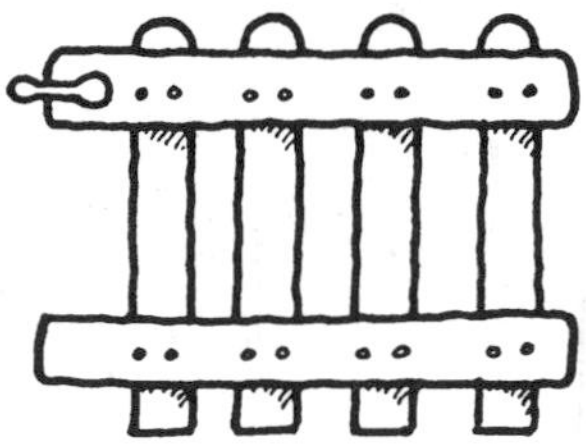 __ate	 __oldfish	 __oat	 __olf
 __ __ue	 __ __ass	 __ __obe	 __ __ove
 __ __ass	 __ __apes	 __ __ave	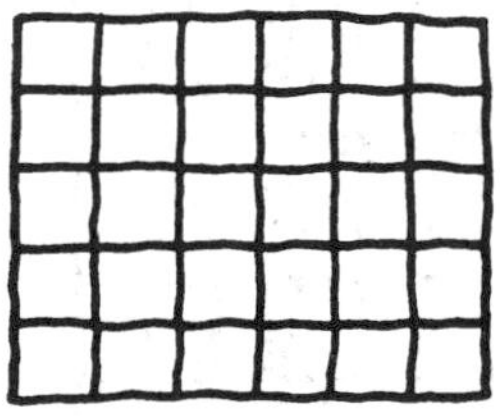 __ __id

- Complete these colours with gr.

__ __een __ __ey

- List things in your classroom which begin with gl, gr or g.

Teachers' note: Introduce the activity with a shared text with **g** words, for example, *Gregory Griggs**. Ask the children to listen for words which begin with **g**. They could think of more of them and then sort them into **gr**, **gl**, and **g** words.

s and s clusters

- **Draw lines to join the pictures to their beginning sounds.**

sp

sw

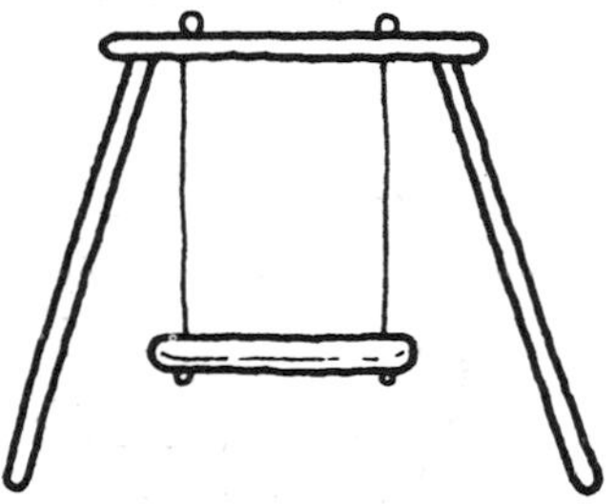

st

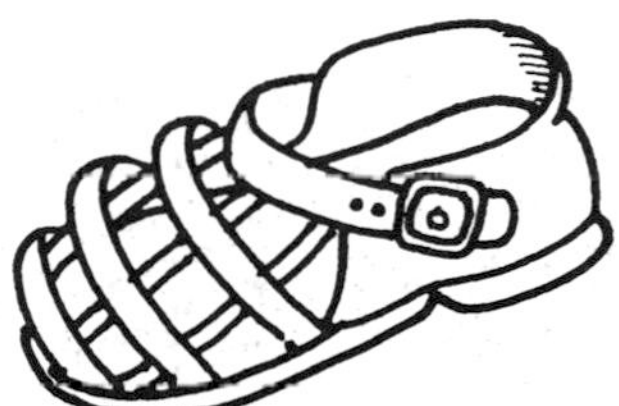

s

- **List the words which begin with sp, sw, st or s.**

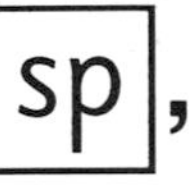   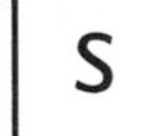

- **In a dictionary, look for words beginning with sp, sw, st and s.**
- **List some of the words you know.**

Teachers' note Introduce the activity with a shared text with **s** words, for example, *Swan Swim**. Ask the children to listen for words which begin with **s**. They could think of more of them and then sort them into **sp, sw, st** and **s** words.

sn sm sk sl clusters

• Draw lines to join the pictures to their beginning sounds.

sn

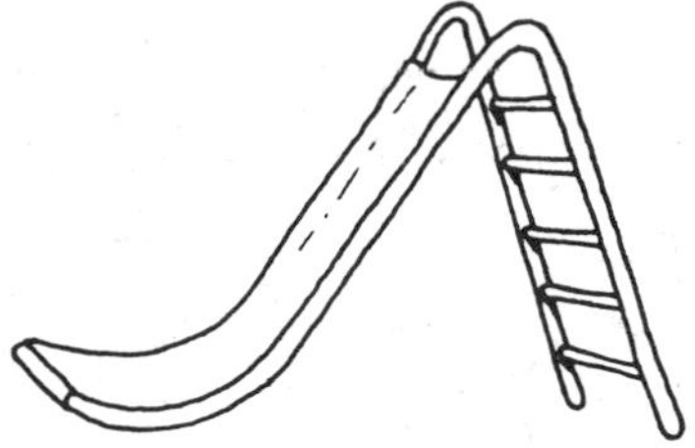

sm

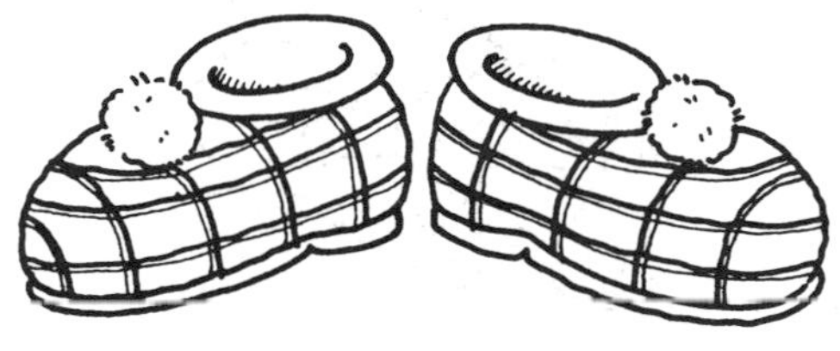

sk

sl

• List the words which begin with 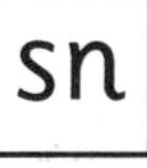 sn,  sm,  sk or sl.

• In a dictionary, look for words beginning with sn, sm, sk and sl.

• List some of the words you know.

Teachers' note During the whole class introduction, read a shared text for exploring words which begin with **s**, such as, *Were going on a bear hunt* by Michael Rosen (Walker Books). During the plenary session, the children could contribute to an **s** word bank in which the words are sorted into columns: **sp, st, sw, sn, sm, sk, sl, s.**

Onset clusters and rime

- Say the words
- Complete the words.
- Circle the beginning sounds.

sp	cr	sk	pl	dr
br	st	sl	fr	sm
bl	gr	sw	tr	cl

plug	_ _ ips	_ _ ing	_ _ ush
_ _ actor	_ _ _ _ _ _	_ _ _ _ _	_ _ _ _ _ _
_ _ _ _ _ _ _ _	_ _ _ _ _ _	_ _ _ _ _	_ _ _ _ _ _ _
_ _ _ _ _ _ _ _	_ _ _ _ _ _ _	_ _ _ _ _ _ _ _	_ _ _ _ _

- With a friend, play 'I spy' with these beginnings.

pl	sk
sw	br
dr	tr
st	sl

Teachers' note Introduce the activity with a set of objects. As the children say the names of the objects, sort them into sets with the same onset cluster and then label the sets with their onsets **pl, dr, sw, br, tr** and so on.